OUTRAGEOUS KINDNESS

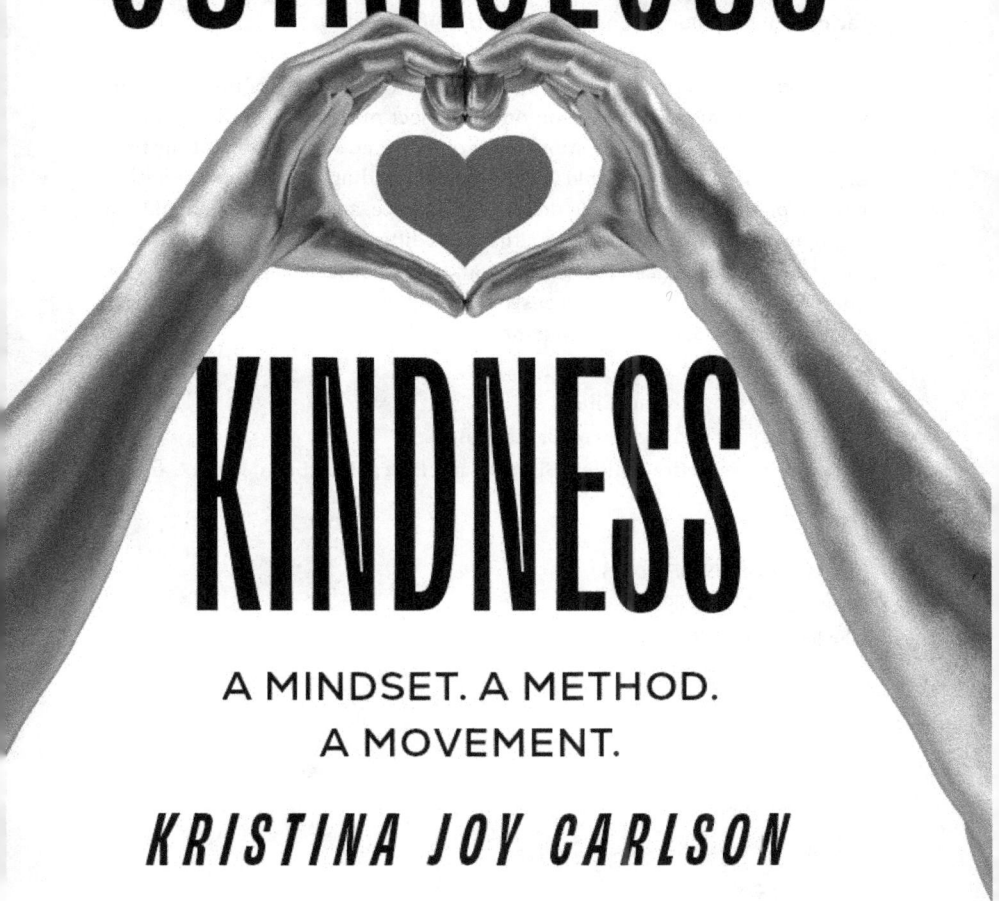

OUTRAGEOUS

KINDNESS

A MINDSET. A METHOD. A MOVEMENT.

KRISTINA JOY CARLSON

OUTRAGEOUS KINDNESS
A Mindset. A Method. A Movement.

Cover Design by Abigael Elliott
Interior Layout and Design by Brittany Becker
Editorial Team: Jeffrey Miller, Ginny Glass, Becca Blackburn, Kiska Carr

ISBNs:
Ebook: 979-8-89165-302-3
Paperback: 979-8-89165-303-0
Hardcover: 979-8-89165-304-7

Published by:
Streamline
Kansas City, MO
shareyourstory.com

Streamline
BOOKS

For Captain

CONTENTS

A Kindness That Can Change the World

HAVE YOU EVER thought, *There has to be more than this*? Or wondered if anything you do really matters—or if you're simply too overwhelmed to make a difference?

I have. Many times, I have wondered how we are still fighting some of the same wars, watching children suffer, hating entire groups of people because of their differences, all the while building more barriers that leave us lonely, disconnected, and unable to achieve meaningful success.

That's not to say there hasn't been progress. Because of the collective action of hundreds of thousands of people who wore pink ribbons, raced for the cure, and raised millions of dollars for research, my breast cancer diagnosis in 2014 was not the death sentence it would have been thirty years before.

Yet it seems so many people have quietly lost hope that what they do makes any real difference. In a world overwhelmed by crisis, division, and exhaustion, kindness can feel like a relic—polite, sweet, but far too passive for the scale of the pain we're up against.

We celebrate megabillionaires for sweeping acts of generosity and global change while the rest of us are left wondering if our efforts matter at all.

But what if we've misunderstood kindness entirely?

What if real kindness isn't soft or sentimental but disruptive?

What if it's the courageous drumbeat of something fierce and transformative?

This is the heart of Outrageous Kindness. A mindset, a method, and a movement.

It is so much more than being "nice." It's about challenging the quiet assumptions that keep us disconnected. It's about showing up when it's inconvenient, listening when it's uncomfortable, and choosing generosity over indifference. It's about reclaiming hope and daring to believe that even small acts of kindness can shake the world.

At its core, Outrageous Kindness invites us to move through life with open eyes, open hearts, and open hands. It asks us to pursue success in a manner that aligns with our values. It calls us to be brave enough to ask for help and bold enough to offer it. It asks us to step off autopilot, pause long enough to notice what's missing, and then do something about it—even if that something feels small.

In the following pages, you'll find stories, reflections, and strategies for how to live with this kind of courageous compassion. From boardrooms to family rooms, from small acts to sweeping initiatives, we'll explore how Outrageous Kindness can transform the way we lead, live, and love.

You'll learn that the world doesn't need more performative gestures. It needs people who are willing to care deeply, act intentionally, and believe relentlessly in the possibility of positive change.

You'll also read about my personal experiences in these pages, but it's about more than me. It's about *us*. About the possibility of a movement rooted in something simple and deeply human: the belief that everyone can make a difference, even through the smallest acts.

My hope is that these words help you stop doubting your capacity to create change. That they help you replace stress with joy, build meaningful connections, repurpose the relentless scroll of social media outrage, and instead step toward meaning—toward a life that feels whole, grounded, and full of purpose.

Because in spite of what our world might tell you, you don't need to be extraordinary to create extraordinary change. You just need to be outrageously kind: one choice, one moment, one connection at a time.

CHAPTER 1

What Is Outrageous Kindness?

THERE'S A KINDNESS crisis in the world today. We live in a time when kindness is often mistaken for weakness and empathy is seen as naive. When, in order to win an argument or feel validated, we're told we have to tear someone else down and dehumanize them. Entire groups of people get reduced to caricatures so we can feel justified in our outrage. We divide, separate, and fragment, *and then* try to build hope on that broken foundation.

The digital world has only intensified this divide. The social media platforms we scroll through daily weren't designed to expand our minds or soften our hearts. They were engineered to feed us more of what we already believe, buy, like, and share. The algorithms reward our preferences, not our growth. They don't encourage us to think differently, to encounter people who see the world another way, or to bridge gaps. Instead, they push us deeper into digital silos and curated bubbles that reflect us back to ourselves, over and over again.

The internet was supposed to make the world bigger. In many ways, it has done the opposite. It has divided our discourse and discouraged our curiosity. More often than not, social media feeds us what some have called "rage bait," content engineered to spark outrage and deepen the "us vs. them" mentality. It's a steady drip of emotional adrenaline that keeps us locked into our feeds and away from each other.

We're also living in what many of my clients in the global humanitarian space describe as a *perma-crisis*. We are inundated with a steady stream of disaster news. One day it's a wildfire, the next a war, the next a new disease, the next a humanitarian breakdown on the other side of the world (or in our own backyard). Crisis after crisis, uncertainty after uncertainty. It's no wonder people are tired, and despair is setting in.

The pressure on women is greater than ever. Old battles are being refought. Lack of resources has added to the pressure of juggling careers, children, caring for parents or grandparents, and maintaining appearances.

And sadly, our youngest generation, which should be bursting with idealism and wild dreams for the future, is statistically the most pessimistic generation ever recorded.[1] They've grown up watching the world unravel. They're not sure if the planet will be livable by the time they grow old, and they don't trust the systems that claim to protect them. They've been handed economic uncertainty and political polarization, and then asked to find their way forward anyway. And they struggle with the mental health challenges created by isolation, loneliness, and lack of connection.

In that kind of environment, it's easy to give up. It's easy to believe that we, as individuals, are powerless. We tell ourselves that the elite 1 percent and big institutions—corporations and governments—control everything. That nothing we do really matters. That kindness is a luxury we can't afford when the world feels like it's burning down.

But that's a lie. Outrageous Kindness is our resistance to hopelessness and the flame that keeps purpose alive in the dark. It is the daily reminder that we still have agency, that we still belong to each other, that we still get to decide how we show up.

This matters *deeply* because when we are constantly flooded with division, suspicion, and judgment, we begin to lose trust. We lose hope, and we lose sight of our shared humanity.

Outrageous Kindness is the counternarrative to rage. It's the practice of refusing to dehumanize and choosing, again and again, to lead with compassion. Outrageous Kindness is not passive. It is not naive. It's a courageous decision to show up differently in a world that too often invites us to disconnect, label, and attack.

It's choosing to say, "I will not let the algorithm write the story of my relationships. I will write a new story through listening and through love in action."

MORE THAN NICENESS

To be clear, Outrageous Kindness isn't just about doing kind things. Rather, it's about fundamentally transforming the way we see the world and how we move through it. It's a call to lead with bold compassion and radical generosity, to have the courage to challenge the invisible norms that hold us back. At its core, Outrageous Kindness invites us to pause and question the deeply ingrained assumptions we carry about others, about ourselves, and about what's possible.

As part of this transformation, we must learn how to *truly ask*. Asking with vulnerability and clarity is how we grow. It's how we connect and change lives. And, yes, this means we have to face our fears, but if we allow fear to dictate our choices, we will never step into the full power of kindness. We will never disrupt the cycles of pain, isolation, and self-protection that keep us from thriving.

This is a call to live with open eyes and an open heart, to replace assumptions with questions and fear with action. It's deciding again and again that love in action is worth the risk. This approach is not merely a sentimental feeling layered onto a busy life. On the contrary, Outrageous Kindness is powerful and active. It takes bold steps and changes lives, starting with our own. And it all begins with the belief that there is inherent value in every human being.

Every person, no matter their circumstances or story, carries something good and meaningful within themselves. When we begin with that recognition, we open ourselves to the radical idea that we all have the power to create positive change.

I'm not necessarily talking about sweeping, heroic acts, though those have their place. The truth is that the small acts of kindness are often harder than the big ones. We show it in how we treat the person bagging our groceries, how we listen to someone we disagree with, how we walk into a meeting and ensure everyone feels seen, heard, and able to contribute. Sometimes, the kindest outcome is simply that you made it through a tough day without letting frustration get the best of you. You chose patience and openness.

Outrageous Kindness means taking action. It's using your social media platform to uplift instead of tear down. It's radical generosity not because you have extra, but because you believe in the ripple effect. What's small to you might be everything to someone else. This is where revolutions begin. They begin not in grand speeches, but in humble, consistent acts of kindness.

During the course of my career, I've sat through more meetings than I can count or recall. However, in almost every meeting, something has always struck me. In a room of, let's say, thirty people, only two or three will engage in real dialogue. The implied message is that those two or three voices matter more than everyone else's. As I've observed this over and over again, I often find myself wondering, *Why are the rest of us here?*

Imagine instead that every person in that meeting had a reason to be there and a voice that mattered. Even in a meeting about something complex—say, nuclear energy—there's a reason for every seat at the table. If I'm in the room, there's something I can offer (though I am not sure what I would contribute to a conversation about nuclear energy). If you're in that room, there's something you can offer. The challenge is to ensure that value is acknowledged and uplifted.

Of course, this isn't just a workplace issue. It's a cultural problem. We move through systems and conversations where only a few are heard while many are present. That's where Outrageous Kindness can quietly but powerfully transform the way we engage.

That's why I say Outrageous Kindness is intentional. Instead of being passive, it actively creates space where people are seen, not sidelined. But it doesn't stop in boardrooms. It shows up in moments that are far more personal.

I remember a season of my life that was particularly difficult. My husband was sick, I was caregiving full-time, raising a child, building a business, and barely holding it together. People with the best of intentions would say, "Make sure you're taking care of yourself." And I'll be honest, I wanted to throw a chair at them.

It's not that I didn't *believe* in self-care, but it felt like one more thing to add to my already unmanageable list. These people meant well, but what I heard was, "Add this to your burden too. You're responsible for self-care, even now." At that moment, kindness didn't feel kind. It felt disconnected from my daily grind. It's the same reason why offering "thoughts and prayers" often falls flat in the aftermath of a tragedy.

Imagine instead the warmth I felt when a friend showed up at my door with dinner. Or someone showed up and said, "I'll do your laundry if you'll let me." Or when a close friend took my son for a movie to give him some joy and give me some personal time. Or a colleague at work said, "Let's restructure your schedule so you don't have to worry about your paycheck while you're going through this."

That is what Outrageous Kindness looks like. It's more than just a pat on the back or a pretty phrase written on a card. It steps into the chaos and offers real relief rather than mere platitudes. It takes the extra step, the inconvenient step, to make someone's world a little lighter, going beyond the socially acceptable to do what's truly life-changing.

Sometimes, it means taking time to listen to a seemingly unpleasant and argumentative coworker, recognizing that their ideas and thoughts have value, or that maybe their day is heavier than ours and they need grace more than we need to be right.

Outrageous Kindness demands that we be strong enough to care in the moments we'd rather look away. We choose connection when separation is easier. We give when it would be more convenient not to, because we want to be the person who *notices* and then *acts.*

This form of kindness takes effort and a lot of courage, but it's what the world is starving for.

THE ORIGIN OF OUTRAGEOUS KINDNESS

People often ask me where the idea for Outrageous Kindness came from, and to be honest, I don't always know how to answer. It's not like there was one lightning-bolt moment. Rather, it has been a gradual unfolding, a weaving together of experiences, lessons, and the extraordinary people who've shaped my life.

If I trace it back, I think of my father. His work focused on helping organizations and ministries secure the resources they needed to do more impactful work. He spent much of his time asking others for support (financial, time, talent). He never saw this as begging, arm-twisting, or a burden. On the contrary, he felt like it was a privilege. He had the privilege of helping people find purpose and give in ways that aligned with their values. That, to him, was meaningful. That kind of alignment between values and action is where the seeds of Outrageous Kindness were planted for me.

Later in life, I found myself helping a mental health center raise private funds to provide critical services that public systems and insurance just didn't cover. I remember sitting in a board meeting discussing strategy. In the room with us was a woman who lived with severe mental illness. She was technically on the board, but she was treated more like a symbol than a colleague. She wasn't asked to contribute, and no one made space for her voice.

And yet, when it came time to actually step out and start raising support, she was the first one to act. Without hesitation, she organized small events in her community, rallied her neighbors, and raised both awareness and funds. The amount of money she raised wasn't groundbreaking, but others became much more generous as a result. Her *outrageously kind* actions demonstrated what so many had missed, that contributing and making change isn't something only the rich can do and value doesn't come with titles.

Outrageous Kindness is also informed by the many opportunities I've had to quit, especially those times when life delivered more challenges than I thought I could handle.

When the dot-com company I founded had financial problems, I faced the possibility of having to cut some really good people from the company, as well as the possible collapse of the whole business. At the time, the stress seemed unbearable. Trying to help, a fellow entrepreneur took me to lunch, and after I almost ruined my salad with tears, shared his own story of facing gut-wrenching decisions. Then, he shared how important it had been for him in those moments to be kind to himself and take time to go do something fun. This planted the seeds of the small *d* in the KIND Method that you will learn about in chapter 7.

Later, when going through chemotherapy and radiation, I found that, strangely, some of my best days weren't about what was happening to *me* at all. They were about what I could do for someone else and staying connected to a purpose beyond myself.

I remember moments when I sat with others going through their own pain, and instead of focusing on my struggle, I focused on theirs. Or times when I used my experience or my time to support organizations doing powerful work. Those moments gave me strength. I wasn't escaping my hardship; I was *transcending* it.

Something beautiful happens when we declare, "I'm going to help. I'm going to reach out. I'm going to do more to make positive change," and then stay connected to that commitment. That energy lifts others and fuels us, too. It fills the soul and brings meaning to even the most difficult days.

I've seen this again and again in my life and the lives of others. In my breast cancer battle, kindness was a lifeline of hope. When I shifted focus from my pain to someone else's need, I felt stronger and more anchored in purpose. It reminded me that no matter what I was going through, I still had something to offer, and that made me feel *more* like myself.

Other moments have shown me that even the tiniest gestures carry power. My son once called me from the airport after being stranded on a trip. He told me, "Mom, I tried your tactic of asking for help and hoping someone would be kind."

Then he laughed and said, "It actually worked way better than yelling at the gate agent."

That was such a small moment, but it stuck with me. In his own way, he affirmed that the concept of Outrageous Kindness makes a difference.

OUTRAGEOUS KINDNESS AND HAPPINESS

In over three decades of work, I've had the opportunity to sit with some of the world's wealthiest individuals. These are people who, by all outward measures, have achieved extraordinary success, yet many of them aren't happy. Despite the accolades and the big bank accounts, they're still searching. Fulfillment eludes them.

Yet I have *never* met an unhappy, *generous* person. The people who are truly content, who radiate peace and purpose, are the ones who have rooted their lives in contribution. They use their resources, time, and energy to make the world better. They don't do it for show or for recognition, but because they know that this is what it means to live well. Generosity creates a kind of joy that no title, trophy, or transaction can ever match.

When I first started working in philanthropy, I had the opportunity to help direct a capital campaign for a heart center in Florida. Quite a few widows were involved in that effort. These women all had similar stories: They had moved to Florida to finally spend time with their career-achieving husbands, only to watch them lose purpose, decline, and suffer heart attacks on the golf course.

Today, wealth advisers tell us that their clients are increasingly asking them for guidance on how to connect their wealth to something more meaningful. In fact, according to 2023 research by the Retirement Coaches Association, 90 percent of retirees believe financial professionals should be helping them with the nonfinancial aspects of retirement. The top nonfinancial issues cited by retirees include coping with a loss of direction or purpose, staying relevant, managing time, dealing with health issues, and staying connected to family and friends.

Yes, they want to live somewhere nice in retirement and not worry about expenses, but they want more than that. As I often say, "Just how much pickleball or golf can you play?" What if instead you built a legacy through Outrageous Kindness?

In the next chapter, you will read about the KIND Method, a guide for turning small, good intentions and everyday choices into powerful tools for purpose-driven success. It's a framework for creating hope even in the face of overwhelming global issues and deeply personal challenges. It turns feelings into *practice* and provides a road map for building a legacy and making positive changes that can be lived out in our daily choices. The KIND Method gives us a lens through which to view every interaction as an opportunity to serve and connect. It is hope turned into action.

THE POWER OF RECOGNIZING EVERYONE'S UNIQUE VALUE

One of the most powerful examples I've seen recently of Outrageous Kindness in action came from a project I was honored to support through my role as managing director of Global Philanthropy at Carter. We were engaged to support Plan International USA on a major campaign called *We Are the Girls*. This was an ambitious initiative that ultimately raised over $200 million to support girls living in some of the most difficult, dangerous, and marginalized environments in the world.

These were girls facing hunger, violence, exploitation, and countless barriers to education and safety. They lived in places where just being a girl could make you a target, where your dreams could be dismissed before you were even allowed to voice them. The scale of the need was heartbreaking, but the generosity from donors—individuals, companies, and foundations—was amazing. Their kindness helped elevate the work in tangible, meaningful ways.

But what made this effort *outrageously* kind wasn't just the fundraising total. At a critical point in the campaign, one of the organizational leaders at Plan USA asked a simple but transformational question: "Why aren't we listening to the girls we're trying to help?"

What would it look like, she wondered, if we shifted the narrative from having to "rescue" the girls to igniting their own power and bringing their voices to the center of the work? To trust them as contributors, not just recipients? To create a process where they weren't being spoken *for*, but where they were speaking and being heard?

Once that door opened, the impact was stunning. The girls were brilliant and full of ideas, and they began contributing to the vision for their own futures. They brought creativity and a deep knowledge of their own communities, showing the flaws of programs that were designed *for* them instead of *with* them, and offering solutions rooted in lived experience—solutions that no external expert could have imagined alone.

As a result, something beautiful happened. Donors became even more inspired to give. It became a true collaboration between people with financial resources and girls with an abundance of *human* resources.

I believe the donors walked away changed. They were more fulfilled and more connected. More in awe of what generosity *really* means when it's paired with deep listening. They gave, yes, but they also received, and what they received was a profound reminder that kindness is not just about rescuing people but *partnering* with them. It's about believing that everyone, no matter where they live, what they've experienced, or how much money they have, has something to bring to the table.

Today, the Plan approach is a growing model in global humanitarian work, building the bridges between those with financial resources and those with other kinds of human capacity for change.

That's the heart of Outrageous Kindness. It's about doing good *with* others, not just *for* them. It's about turning every interaction into a collaboration that honors dignity and invites everyone to participate in the story of change.

When we do that, the results are always richer and more lasting than we ever imagined.

OUTRAGEOUS KINDNESS AND THE POWER TO CHANGE

Outrageous Kindness strengthens our sense of agency. Every day brings distractions and discouragement: someone's bad attitude, a canceled plan, a frustrating news headline. Any of it can pull us off course, but Outrageous Kindness helps us return to center. It helps us reclaim the moment.

Years ago, when I had the privilege of working on Habitat for Humanity International's first global campaign, I got to witness this firsthand through the work of the founders, Linda and Millard Fuller, and former United States President Jimmy Carter. I remember something President Carter often said, "What distinguishes someone who is *truly* rich from someone who is poor is that a rich person believes they can create change."

He would go on to emphasize that the families receiving the homes were just as "rich" as those helping to build them. That belief, knowing internally that you and everyone around you can make a difference, is real wealth. Every one of us has that capacity, and Outrageous Kindness is the way we unlock it. In that sense, we are all wealthy. We all have the power to create change.

Of course, not all change is positive. You can walk into a room with a bad attitude and drain everyone's energy. You've created change, just not the kind that lifts others. But Outrageous Kindness calls us to higher ground. It invites us to be intentional in using our influence and our words to shape the world around us for the better.

When Outrageous Kindness becomes a societal value, basic human rights are more likely to be honored. Barriers that once seemed permanent begin to crumble. We stop accepting broken systems as inevitable, and we start asking deeper questions. We begin to say, "This isn't good enough—not for me, not for my neighbor, not for the next generation."

Recently, while working with a client, I came across a study that shocked me. It ranked social mobility in major US cities.[2] On that list, Atlanta, Georgia, a place I've always seen as vibrant, full of culture and promise, ranked fifty out of fifty. Dead last. In a city home to the 1996 Olympics, Coca-Cola, Delta Airlines, and some of the biggest movie production studios in the country, 95 percent of children born in poverty will *never* escape it. Ninety-five percent. That is staggering, and that is why Outrageous Kindness matters.

When we truly embrace it, we start to say, "That's not acceptable." We begin to question the assumptions we've made about people and their potential. We admit that maybe there's something we don't know, and we start *listening*.

Outrageous Kindness dares us to ask different questions and imagine different outcomes. It is a bold refusal to look away, and it begins with one person—one act—one choice at a time.

We stop talking *at* each other and start listening to one another. We create spaces for engagement, especially across differences. We dig deeper and ask, "Where are the real barriers? What haven't we seen yet? Who haven't we heard from?"

Businesses that embrace Outrageous Kindness at this level also achieve better results. I've worked with leaders across numerous industries, and one thing I've noticed again and again is that the higher someone rises, the more isolated they often become. The more successful they are, the more difficult it is for others to challenge them, offer dissent, or new ideas. Strategy can go awry, and productivity can suffer. Real, courageous kindness has the power to break through that. It helps leaders stay open and teachable, and it invites them to lead differently and build stronger teams.

PUT YOUR OWN OXYGEN MASK ON FIRST

If I'm being honest, I have to admit I don't always practice what I preach. Even as I sat down to write this book, I wrestled with my own inner barriers. I thought, *Who am I to write about Outrageous Kindness?* I'm not perfect. I lose my patience. I doubt myself. I don't always show up the way I want to.

The truth is, before we can offer Outrageous Kindness to others, we have to offer it to ourselves. There's a voice inside that says, *You're not good enough. You're too old. You're too young. You're too late. You're too much.* It's relentless, and if we let it, it will talk us out of everything good we were ever meant to do.

In his classic book on performance, *The Inner Game of Tennis: The Classic Guide to the Mental Side of Peak Performance*, Tim Gallwey writes about our two selves. Self One is the "teller," constantly giving instructions and judging, while Self Two is the "doer," capable of performing actions. Self One gets in the way for high-performing athletes for sure, but it can get in our way too.

Cultural norms and expectations can add fuel to this inner storm of unkindness. I once had a boss dismiss my relentless work on a project that met its deadline and far surpassed its revenue goal by saying, "You were only able to do that because the board members think you're pretty." In a world that places so much value on how women look (according to *Forbes*, in 2023 alone, the beauty industry made $570 billion in worldwide revenue[3]), you can imagine how hard it was to shut out this phrase and replace it with a narrative that instead emphasized the winning strategy I developed, the hard work I put into building the right team, and my passion for the project.

Extending Outrageous Kindness inward is the first step. You can't change the world until you believe that you are worthy of being part of the change, and that begins with how you talk to yourself. Stop waiting for perfection, and stop needing permission. Stop comparing yourself and start healing. See your own value and change that inner voice. Be outrageously kind to you.

We hear it every time we board a plane: "If the oxygen masks drop down, put your own mask on first before assisting others." And yet, how often do we actually apply that wisdom to our daily lives?

I was talking with my personal trainer recently. During our session, we got into a conversation about how important it is to know what fills your tank and restores your energy. For him, it's dirt biking. If he starts the week without knowing when he's going to get out on his bike, he gets grumpy. Even though he loves his work and the people he works with, something changes in him when that personal joy is missing. He's off balance. His generosity dries up.

As he put it, "You can't feed others if you haven't fed yourself."

If we don't take care of ourselves, it becomes nearly impossible to show up with genuine kindness for others. Instead, we find ourselves running on fumes, snapping at the people we love, saying yes when we mean no, or offering help that feels more like an obligation than grace.

Sometimes the hardest part of self-care isn't knowing what you need—it's admitting that you can't do it alone. When life feels like a big burden, even small acts of care can feel like too much. That's when Outrageous Kindness requires another brave act: *asking for help*. That, too, is kindness—to let others step in, to lean on their strength when yours runs low. It's not weakness but community, and it's how we make sure no one gets left behind in the name of self-sufficiency.

Think about what usually happens during the holiday season. Women, in particular, are often the emotional architects of holiday magic. They plan the meals, buy the gifts, organize the travel, make things special for coworkers, family, friends, neighbors—all while trying to maintain their jobs, their homes, their health, their sanity. They're expected to do it all, and to do it with a smile. God forbid they gain five pounds in the process.

We've created a culture where stress is expected, even celebrated, especially when it's tied to service. But if all that effort doesn't bring you joy, then kindness becomes another box to check and another weight to carry.

This isn't just about the holidays. It's about every season of life. The hustle, the striving, the constant care for others—none of it is sustainable if it doesn't include being kind and generous to yourself. This inner focus isn't selfish. On the contrary, it's the most generous thing you can do because when you are whole, rested, nourished, your kindness becomes real. Your energy becomes a gift instead of a performance.

Outrageous Kindness means giving yourself permission to rest. It means asking yourself what fills you and then fiercely protecting that. Research consistently shows that helping others and engaging in acts of generosity are strongly linked to increased feelings of well-being and happiness. These actions trigger the release of feel-good chemicals in the brain, such as serotonin, dopamine, and oxytocin, which positively impact mood and overall health.

So, yes, put your own mask on first. You can't save anyone if you're gasping for air, and the world needs you strong, joyful, and whole.

CHAPTER 2

Introducing the KIND Method

HOW DOES OUTRAGEOUS Kindness create purpose-driven success and lasting change? It has to be more than something we sprinkle into our days when it's convenient or easy. True life-changing kindness is intentional. It's courageous, and it is *outrageous* in the best possible way. But living with that level of impact requires more than a good heart—it requires a road map.

That's where the KIND Method comes in.

At its core, the KIND Method is a framework that transforms values and good intentions into a plan of action that delivers measurable results. It's not rigid or prescriptive. It's a living, breathing process that adapts to the realities of life.

Through decades of working with leaders, teams, and organizations, we've discovered that there is no single, perfect path to change. No one-size-fits-all way to achieve a dream, produce triple bottom line business results, transform a community, or improve your own life. Circumstances evolve. Obstacles arise. Even the best-laid plans are met with unexpected challenges. Some changes you can anticipate; others you can't.

The KIND Method was born from the need to stay anchored to purpose while being flexible enough to learn and adapt as the world around us changes so we can make meaningful progress anyway.

It offers a way to navigate uncertainty without losing sight of your goals. A way to turn kindness from a random act into a sustainable, transformational force in your life and the lives of others. Outrageous Kindness isn't about doing one good deed and walking away. It's about building a life where kindness is woven into everything you do, with consistency and courage.

The KIND Method helps individuals, teams, and organizations to define key things:

- What outcome are we striving for?
- How will we get there?
- What more do we need to understand, what else must we learn, and who do we still need to engage or build relationships with?
- How will we adjust along the way?

Without these answers, even the best intentions can float away, lost to busyness or frustration. With them, kindness becomes a powerful force for growth, healing, hope, and success.

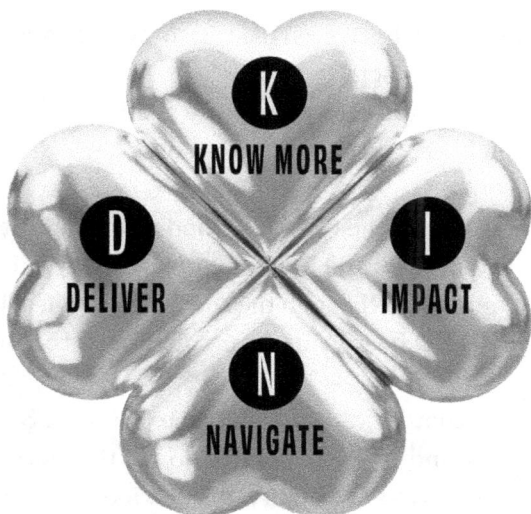

HOW THE KIND METHOD CAME TO LIFE

The KIND Method wasn't developed in a laboratory or dreamed up overnight. It grew from decades of building businesses and hands-on work alongside generous leaders and purpose-driven organizations. We saw time and time again that good intentions are not enough.

If good intentions alone could change the world, none of us would need a road map. We would simply wish for change and watch it happen. But real change demands courage, resilience, and a framework for action.

Across all our experiences, while every situation was different, a few timeless truths revealed themselves:

- Change is always harder than it looks from a distance.
- Dreams drift without direction.

- Values must be translated into action plans to have real-world impact.
- Fear and complacency are fierce enemies.
- Passion is necessary and contagious.

From these truths, the KIND Method took shape. It's a framework designed not to stifle individuality or rigidly dictate every move, but to guide you through the storms, help you adjust course when needed, and keep your heart anchored to your greater purpose.

It exists so that kindness isn't left to chance. So that your values, dreams, and desire to create good in the world can move from hopeful ideas to lived reality. When kindness is purposeful, it is unstoppable.

The KIND Method can be a powerful corporate strategy or a professional tool. It's also deeply personal.

The framework we teach today was born not only from decades of professional work—guiding leaders, building purpose-driven teams, and helping organizations navigate change—but also from the moments life brought us to our knees. It was forged in boardrooms, yes, but also in moments of trauma and sheer terror.

FLY THE PLANE

I remember one such moment vividly. I was flying in a small airplane, holding my baby, when we hit a violent storm. In an instant, the plane nosedived. The pilot, my late husband, busied himself trying to reach air traffic control on the radio, seeking help.

Everything in me wanted to panic. To scream. To lose control. And honestly, no one would have blamed me if I had. The plane was almost completely vertical. But in that split second, another instinct rose up—the instinct to find a solution, to *be* the calm that the situation so desperately needed.

I knew that if I gave in to fear, it would only make the situation harder. So instead, I focused. I anchored myself in the hope of a good outcome. I breathed for myself and for the tiny life depending on me, and I calmly said, "Fly the plane. Fly the plane. Fly the plane." There was nothing more to do. Air traffic control could not help us.

I knew making sure we were ready to recover when the downdraft ended would make a huge difference, and I wanted my husband to hear me say I had confidence in his ability to get us through this life-threatening moment. Instead of giving in to fear, by saying "fly the plane," I conveyed to him: "You have the skills, talent, and mental focus to do this."

We broke through the clouds at about a hundred feet above the ground, and the downdraft finally let us go. It took a few more moments to find a safe flight path, but believe me: We immediately focused on finding a place to land. It wasn't until we were safely on the ground that we took the time to call air traffic control again. They were relieved to hear from us.

That experience, and others like it, forever shaped how I see resilience, leadership, and kindness in action. Now, when circumstances seem out of my control, "fly the plane" has become a rallying cry for bringing my focus back to what matters and what I can do.

The KIND Method keeps finding new ways to be applied in the stability of boardrooms and also in the stormy, scary moments of real life. It's about learning how to stay rooted in purpose even when the world feels like it's falling apart. It's about creating positive outcomes—not just when everything is going well, but especially when it's not. That's where real leadership is tested—when stakes are high, uncertainty looms, and people are watching to see how you'll respond.

Throughout my life and career, I've had the privilege of witnessing countless leaders navigating layoffs, leading through natural disasters, steering through personal heartbreaks—all while continuing to deliver hope and progress for the people who counted on them.

The KIND Method is shaped by all of these experiences. It's a blueprint not just for thriving in good times, but for overcoming in the hard times with kindness and purpose.

A FRAMEWORK AND A MOVEMENT

At the center of the KIND Method is a simple acronym: *K-I-N-D*. Each letter represents a key element of the journey from good intentions to transformational success.

Here's a high-level overview of the KIND Method framework:

Know More

Every change, every act of kindness, begins with a recognition that your perception, experiences, and knowledge are incomplete. Knowing more means having an openness to developing a new lens through active listening, deep self-awareness, thoughtful data, and meaningful insight. It's about paying attention—to yourself, to others, and to the world around you—and letting that awareness guide your actions.

Impact

Impact is the heart of purpose. It's about defining the change you seek and building systems that allow you to track, measure, and scale it. Purpose without direction can get lost. Impact means getting clear about what you want to change—in your life, in your business or community, or in the world—and putting structures in place to make that change real.

Navigate

In a world that seems to shift beneath our feet daily, the ability to adapt with intention is incredibly important. Navigate reminds us to use our purpose and values as a compass, steering through complexity without losing our way. Change is inevitable. The question is, can we move through it with grace, persistence, and clarity? Navigate equips us to do exactly that.

Deliver

At the end of the day, action is what transforms dreams into results. Deliver is about turning strategy into milestones and milestones into sustained success and stronger relationships. It's about bold, consistent movement toward the outcomes we envision, because kindness without action is just a wish.

Each piece of the framework builds on the one before it. Knowledge informs impact. Impact guides navigation. Navigation enables delivery. And together, they create a cycle of purposeful Outrageous Kindness that leads to lasting change and meaningful legacies.

You can apply the KIND Method to deeply personal challenges, such as healing a broken relationship, finding forgiveness, or leading your family through a season of change. Or you can apply it to major organizational efforts, like reimagining a company's culture, guiding a nonprofit toward greater impact, or leading a team to drive toward better outcomes.

The principles are the same, but the process is flexible, adaptable to the needs and complexities of real life.

We offer worksheets, tools, and methodologies to help along the way, but they are never rigid checklists. The real work happens inside you, as you open your mind, adapt to change, and lead with unwavering kindness. We don't believe in a one-size-fits-all, check-the-box approach to anything. We don't believe you have to do it *our* way to do it the *right* way.

Instead, the KIND Method meets you where you are, in the real, messy, beautiful complexity of your life, and offers a flexible framework you can adapt to your needs, goals, and circumstances. That's why:

- We provide guidance, not mandates.
- We offer resources, not rules.
- We invite adaptation, not rigid compliance.

This flexibility is important because Outrageous Kindness cannot be formulaic. It must be authentic, responsive, and rooted in your unique purpose.

A Commitment to Outrageous Kindness

Our goal is to ignite a movement of a million people or more, all aligned around one mission: to flood the world with purposeful, transformational kindness. At the heart of this journey is a commitment—a bold and unapologetic choice to lead with kindness, no matter the circumstance. Kindness that isn't timid or per-formative, but fierce, courageous, and life-changing.

This commitment is captured in the Outrageous Kindness Pledge:

OUTRAGEOUS KINDNESS PLEDGE

◊ *I pledge to lead with kindness—boldly, bravely, and without apology.*
◊ *I will pursue outrageous goals with compassion—for others and for myself.*
◊ *I will seek fresh perspective, act with purpose, and choose kindness, even when it's hard, inconvenient, or unexpected.*
◊ *Outrageous Kindness is the difference I choose to make.*

This is a pledge to be kind not only when it's easy or when we feel like it. It's about embodying kindness when it's hard, inconvenient, or countercultural. It's a commitment to stepping forward with heart, hope, and conviction, to be a difference-maker in a world that desperately needs it.

CHAPTER 3

K—Know More

AT THE VERY heart of the KIND Method, and at the root of Outrageous Kindness itself, is the commitment to know more.

This is about more than simply gathering facts. It's about opening our minds and hearts to the likelihood that the way we currently perceive things may not be the full picture. In fact, it often isn't.

I've always loved movies like *Gone Girl* and *Pulp Fiction* and books like *James* by Percival Everett, not just for their storytelling brilliance, but for what they reveal about perspective. In films and books like these, you experience the same event multiple times but through different characters' eyes. What you first believe to be true is turned on its head when you see it from another angle. At first, you're convinced you know what happened. But then, another layer is revealed. Another story is told. And suddenly you realize, maybe you didn't understand it as fully as you thought.

Outrageous Kindness means embracing the humility to admit we don't know everything, having the courage to seek fresh perspectives, and being willing to challenge our own assumptions.

My late husband had a saying I often return to: "There are three sides to every story—yours, mine, and probably what really happened."

As an example, in June 2025, people took to the streets of Los Angeles to voice their objection to the manner in which the United States government was looking for undocumented people. With friends and business associates in the area, I was more than curious to try to understand what was happening. I spent an evening watching and reading every account of the situation that I could find. Soon, I discovered that, depending on the source, this was either

- a peaceful protest by good people exercising their right to free speech and assembly;
- a violent protest by insurgents;
- the rise of a fascist police state and the further demise of democracy;
- some combination of the above; or
- none of the above.

Only time will tell which is the "real" story. But it is a good reminder of the importance of listening to other voices. To practice Outrageous Kindness, we must recognize that truth is often layered. We need fresh perspectives and fresh data. We need to listen to voices beyond our own experience. Only then can we unlock the best in ourselves and the best in others.

This principle is not just personal; it is transformational at the societal level. Research, including groundbreaking work from Erica Chenoweth at the Harvard Kennedy School, has shown that real, sustained change doesn't happen through force or by silencing opposition. It happens when people with differing views find common ground, when they agree to disagree on some things in order to move forward together on others.[4]

Outrageous Kindness thrives not by demanding uniformity, but by building unlikely alliances and honoring different experiences. It's a commitment to seek understanding before judgment.

BREAKING THROUGH THE CULTURE OF ASSUMPTIONS

One of the biggest barriers to Outrageous Kindness is *the culture of assumptions*. Too often, what stands in the way of bold kindness and outrageous goals isn't a lack of desire. It's the unexamined assumptions we carry about other people, about the data we see, about what's possible or impossible.

We assume we know someone's story. We assume the obstacles are immovable. We assume kindness won't matter, or worse, that it will make us vulnerable. These assumptions cloud our vision. They close our hearts and prevent us from seeing the opportunities for connection, growth, and change that are right in front of us.

Breaking down the culture of assumptions is necessary if we are to practice Outrageous Kindness in any lasting, world-changing way. That's why the first step in the KIND Method is so critically important. When we listen deeper, ask better questions, and stay curious instead of judgmental, we unlock the true power of kindness.

In today's world, where social media algorithms often feed us only the ideas we already agree with, committing to "know more" is harder than ever. The digital spaces we inhabit are designed to reinforce our existing views, not to challenge them.

That's why choosing to seek out fresh perspectives is a deliberate act of courage.

When we work with leaders inside organizations, we often find that even their inner circles unintentionally limit the flow of new ideas. Well-meaning teams manage the information that reaches the leader, sometimes protecting them so carefully that open dialogue becomes nearly impossible.

My friend and cofounder of Outrageous Kindness, LLC, Susan Boyette, and I have laughed (and sometimes sighed) at how often we've seen this, even among world-renowned leaders. Without realizing it, the people around them filter and shape the narrative, leaving little room for voices who might offer a new or challenging perspective. Yet, those are exactly the voices who drive innovation, healing, and lasting change.

In one such instance, a world-renowned CEO was sitting in the room with his closest team members as we were discussing his leadership of a major charitable campaign. As the conversation unfolded, something odd began to happen. Every time a question was directed at the CEO, someone on his team would jump in to answer, speaking for him, as if shielding him rather than engaging him.

It happened again and again until finally, after several rounds of this, one of our colleagues leaned forward, paused just long enough for the discomfort to settle, and said, "Shouldn't we ask him? He's in the room."

This happens so often. In his book, *Think Again: The Power of Knowing What You Don't Know*, Adam Grant describes the four different ways we respond to ideas, especially with teams or groups:

- The *preacher* pushes ideas, convinced of their rightness and expecting others to believe things on sheer faith.

- The *politician* seeks the approval of others before acting, much like the senior leaders in the story above.
- The *prosecutor* builds "sides," tries to prove what is "right," and demonstrates the wrongness of others.
- The *scientist*, however, approaches everything as a question to be answered. They want to know more and are willing to change their stance when new information is available. Being more like a scientist is essential to breaking down cultures of assumptions and practicing Outrageous Kindness.

I would add to the list that some people respond as a fourth *p* and become *procrastinators*. Not wanting conflict, they tune it all out and wait to see if anything will really change.

Know more means intentionally creating spaces in our work, our communities, and in our own lives where diverse voices can be heard. Where fresh ideas are welcomed. Where disagreement isn't seen as a threat, but as an opportunity for growth. On a personal level, this shows up in the small moments. When you meet someone who doesn't look like you, doesn't act like you, or comes from circumstances you can barely imagine—do you lean in with curiosity or recoil with judgment?

It's so easy to make quick assumptions about who someone is or what they're capable of, but Outrageous Kindness asks us to pause and wonder instead of assume. To seek understanding instead of rushing to judgment. Practicing outrageous kindness at this level is an act of deep respect, both for others and for yourself. It's an acknowledgment of the inherent dignity and value that lives inside every person.

I often see this challenge arise in my work coaching women entrepreneurs. There's a real temptation to seek out only those who affirm us, who agree with our dreams and our plans. While positive energy and encouragement are important, real growth happens when we allow space for constructive challenge.

When I launched my first business, my earliest financial investors were angels—friends and colleagues who were already fans. They offered much-needed initial capital but little in the way of constructive criticism of the business plan. Things changed quickly when we started seeking out venture capital from institutional investors. I soon got an education on everything that was wrong with the business strategy. It was tough, but it revealed some blind spots I hadn't seen before and also helped uncover new opportunities.

This willingness to learn and listen to those who see the world differently is not easy.

Not shying away from hard conversations but stepping into them takes courage, compassion, and a heart wide open to what more there is to know. Because knowing more isn't just a mindset, it's the first act of real, revolutionary kindness. After all, as I did with my first business venture, we often learn more from the people who reject our ideas than from those who embrace them.

It's often where we find real growth too—the kind that fuels both innovation and kindness.

Practicing Outrageous Kindness means embracing the uncomfortable fact that our assumptions might be standing in our way. It means recognizing that what we "know" is not the whole story.

We've seen it firsthand in multiple circumstances.

- Assumptions have weakened critical relationships.
- Assumptions have stunted innovation and collaboration.
- Assumptions have created toxic work cultures.
- Assumptions have stymied fundraising results.
- Assumptions have derailed sales revenue goals.
- Assumptions have stood in the way of breaking cycles of generational poverty.

When people act based on what they *think* they know, without seeking fresh insight, they limit what's possible. Again and again, assumptions have proven to be one of the biggest silent barriers to meaningful progress in business, in relationships, and within ourselves.

That's why the *K* in KIND is so foundational to Outrageous Kindness. We must question what we think we know, seeking out other perspectives, and committing to active learning as a daily practice. Think of it like a muscle: The more we use it, the more we ask, listen, seek, and challenge—the stronger it becomes. And the more naturally that Outrageous Kindness can flow through us and from us.

I'll never forget a conversation I had with a nonprofit CEO who had been struggling to connect with a major donor. "She's just not interested anymore," he said. "She's moved on." When I asked if he'd reached out recently—*really* reached out—he admitted it had been months. He'd assumed her silence meant she didn't care. I nudged him to try again, with curiosity but no agenda.

Two weeks later, I got an email from him with the subject line: "You were right." It turned out the donor's husband had been gravely ill, and she'd been quietly stepping back from everything, including philanthropy. When he reached out with empathy instead of expectation, she opened up and thanked him for seeing her as a person, not just a line item. They had a stronger relationship as a result, and ultimately, she returned to being a very generous contributor to the organization.

That's the power of questioning what we think we know. When we set aside our assumptions and lead with presence and care, we open the door to connection and impact that goes far beyond what we imagined.

THE CHALLENGE OF CHANGING BEHAVIOR

When my family made the decision to leave Atlanta and settle in Oxford, Mississippi, we were drawn to the small-college-town charm. It seemed like a wonderful place for our son to grow up. Still, the transition wasn't easy. I missed many of the conveniences and variety the big city offered—from grocery stores and restaurants to doctors and churches. But what I missed most was my fitness community.

In Atlanta, the friends and peers who shared my commitment to a healthy lifestyle did more than just help me fit into my skinny jeans. (And let me tell you: When that zipper doesn't want to budge, the self-talk gets rough.)

So, I did what any normal person would do (not): I got certified to teach Gyrotonic, Pilates, and barre, recruited others to do the same, and opened a fitness studio—Ice Core Fitness.

In the early months of the business, I spent a lot of time simply trying to explain why a different approach to exercise was necessary. More than a few people took a class or two and decided it "didn't work." They came in with assumptions—that exercise should be a quick fix for last night's overindulgence or a crash plan to get ready for a wedding. Few saw it as a lifestyle change, much less a community.

Opening minds and building that community became one of the most important and rewarding parts of the business. It took daily effort. We offered more than just classes and instruction. We also introduced nutrition workshops, created space for social connection, and encouraged a holistic view of wellness. Slowly but surely, our regulars began to experience real, lasting changes in both their health and their sense of belonging.

So much so that, even after I sold the business in 2015, the community that grew from Ice Core Fitness remains one of my greatest treasures. We may not see each other as often, but we still show up for each other.

Changing behavior is difficult, whether within ourselves or within an organization. Often, the greatest resistance we face doesn't come from hard facts but from assumptions. We make assumptions about who people are, why they act the way they do, and how they will respond. We convince ourselves that we know more than we do about colleagues, customers, events, even friends and family.

This is human nature, but why are we so prone to assume instead of inquire?

Because uncertainty is deeply uncomfortable.

Research shows that people experience greater stress from *not knowing* than from facing a negative certainty.[5] In a 2016 study published in *Nature Communications*, researchers found that people who had a 50 percent chance of receiving an electric shock experienced *more* stress than those who knew they were definitely going to get shocked. That may seem surprising, but it goes to show that when we don't know what's coming, we suffer more.

Uncertainty is deeply uncomfortable, and there's a reason for that. Our brains aren't wired to love ambiguity. The brain craves clarity. In the absence of clear answers, we fill in the blanks with assumptions to ease our discomfort. Instead of seeking new perspectives, we lean on what we think we already understand.

That's not weakness. It's biology. Psychologists Kruglanski and Webster gave this discomfort a name back in 1994: *the need for cognitive closure*. Human beings crave definite answers. When we don't get them, we grow frustrated, impatient, and anxious. And in that emotional state, we're far more likely to lean on easy assumptions and quick judgments instead of seeking deeper understanding.

Personally, we tend to surround ourselves with people who agree with us.

Professionally, we often build teams that reflect and reinforce our own views.

Digitally, social media algorithms filter our experiences even further, showing us more of what we already believe and less of what might challenge us.

All of this makes it even harder to break out of the closed loops we live in. The problem is that unchecked assumptions stifle progress. They limit innovation and undermine relationships, and, perhaps most importantly, they block the transformational power of kindness.

If we truly want to practice Outrageous Kindness—if we want to lead, grow, and connect in powerful ways—we must be willing to break the culture of assumptions. How do we do that? First, by admitting that we don't have all the answers. Then, by making a commitment to seek new ones. This requires openness, humility, and a relentless curiosity about the world beyond our own experiences.

Let me share a simple, real-world example of how assumptions, left unchallenged, can quietly limit our potential to create change.

In a recent meeting, the chief operating officer of a large international organization insisted that their donors should not be asked to give beyond their current contributions. His reasoning was, "They already give all they can."

At first glance, it seemed like a compassionate, reasonable assumption, but when we looked at the data, a very different picture emerged. The numbers revealed that there was significant potential for increased support. Despite this fact, the COO resisted, and many others in the room agreed with him.

Why would he resist, even in the face of data? Because often, when people insist they know how others will act, they are unconsciously revealing something about themselves. *They* don't want to be asked for more and are uncomfortable with the idea of stretching, so they project their own limits onto others.

In this case, the assumption wasn't about the donors at all. It was about the leaders' own internal barriers. Since no one challenged it, opportunities were left unexplored. Generosity that might have been awakened was never even invited.

This is how uncertainty fuels resistance. When leaders feel unsure about outcomes, when fear creeps in, when doubt clouds judgment, they often fall back on quick, familiar narratives. They say things like "People won't want that," "They'll say no," and "It's too much to ask."

Research shows that uncertainty drains our mental energy. A 2021 study in *The Journal of Experimental Psychology* showed how constant ambiguity can lead to *decision fatigue*—a state where even the strongest leaders start rushing decisions, oversimplifying problems, and avoiding creative solutions.[6] It's not because they don't care. It's because their brains are tired.

When that happens, we default to assumptions rather than doing the harder but more fruitful work of exploration. Instead of leaning into curiosity, we lean into comfort. Instead of asking, we assume. Instead of expanding possibilities, we quietly shrink them. And every time we allow assumptions to go unchallenged, we limit what is possible, not just for ourselves but for the people and causes we hope to serve.

In other words, when we don't know what's going on, we instinctively try to close the gap with assumptions. It's not because we're lazy, but because our nervous systems are wired to seek relief.

The impact of uncertainty shows up everywhere, but especially in the workplace. According to the American Psychological Association, employees who experience unclear leadership or a lack of direction report higher levels of stress, lower engagement, and greater resistance to change.[7]

This is where Outrageous Kindness invites us to something higher. Kindness doesn't just show up in moments of confidence and clarity. It shines most brightly in the fog of the unknown. And one of the kindest, bravest things we can do in the face of uncertainty is also one of the simplest: *ask*.

ERASING ASSUMPTIONS AT GEORGIA STATE

One of the most inspiring examples I know comes from Georgia State University, a school that has become a national model for helping minority and first-generation college students not only enroll but also graduate in record numbers.

Susan Boyette, my Outrageous Kindness partner and longtime colleague, often points to Georgia State University as one of the most compelling examples of kindness meeting innovation in higher education. She knows the institution well, having both studied there and later served as the associate vice president for the Burning Bright Capital Campaign. For Susan, Georgia State isn't just a school; it's a living, evolving example of what happens when we stop assuming and start listening with compassion.

Georgia State's main campus is located in the heart of downtown Atlanta, surrounded by underserved neighborhoods where opportunity is hard-won. Many of the students entering Georgia State were the first in their families to go to college. Some had never set foot inside an office building, had never had a formal conversation about finances, and had little experience navigating the kind of bureaucratic systems higher education depends on.

At first, like many institutions, Georgia State made the mistake of assuming these students would simply know how to handle the admissions and enrollment process. They expected students to have ready access to documents like birth certificates or Social Security numbers, or to easily answer questions like "Where was your father born?" But for many students, those requests were anything but simple. Some didn't know where their birth certificates were. Others didn't know if their fathers were alive. Many carried invisible burdens—histories of loss, poverty, incarceration, or instability. The system, as it was built, expected them to clear these hurdles without pause or support.

But then Georgia State did something remarkable. They stopped assuming and started asking a better question: *What if we meet every student exactly where they are?*

Instead of blaming students for struggling, they built systems that anticipated those struggles. They used technology—chatbots, customized application flows, proactive outreach—to guide students quietly and compassionately through complex paperwork. They removed shame and confusion, creating a space where a student could say, "I don't have that," and be met not with judgment but with help.

And it didn't stop there. The university also uncovered a troubling trend: A significant number of students who were close to graduating—sometimes just a class or two away—were dropping out. The reason, they found, was often due to small unpaid balances. A parking ticket. A $400 fee. The old mindset was, "They'll find a way to pay and come back." But too often, they didn't. Life intervened, and their dreams got sidelined.

So, Georgia State changed their approach again. They created systems to track student balances and intervene *before* those balances became barriers. When a student faced a financial snag, the university stepped in with microgrants. It was small money with a huge impact. To launch this effort in 2011, then-president Mark Becker gave a generous lead gift to establish the Panther Retention Fund, which is now a nationally recognized initiative that has helped thousands of students stay in school and graduate.[8]

Perhaps most radically, Georgia State normalized the idea that students don't just need academic instruction—they need life coaching, system navigation, and emotional support. They even created an immersive month-long onboarding experience where students could ask questions, build confidence, and learn the basics before classes began.

As I reflect on Georgia State's evolution, I see Outrageous Kindness in action, the kind that stops expecting perfection and starts designing for reality. What started as an act of stepping back and questioning assumptions has now become a national model for student success. Colleges across the country have begun adopting Georgia State's approach, recognizing that true kindness in education means refusing to assume, and instead, choosing to know more.

When you erase assumptions and build systems rooted in *knowing* and understanding, you don't just change individual lives. You change futures. You change communities. You change the world.

One of the reasons I love the Georgia State story so much is that it beautifully captures a truth we often overlook: It's easy to make assumptions. It's easy to imagine we understand why a first-generation student succeeds or struggles in college. It's easy to come up with neat, simple answers about why someone from a certain background does or doesn't attend school. What Georgia State did was remarkable. Instead of buying into those assumptions, they went out and got the data. They listened and observed, and they committed to understanding what the real barriers were.

Instead of settling for easy answers, they pushed deeper to uncover what was truly standing in the way of success. That kind of relentless curiosity is at the heart of Outrageous Kindness.

Real kindness isn't about assuming we know someone else's story. It's about having the humility to admit that we don't, and the courage to seek true understanding instead.

While college success is certainly important, the bigger lesson here is universal. Whatever challenges we're trying to address in our communities, our relationships, or even within ourselves, we must be willing to lay down our assumptions and truly listen, observe, and learn. That spirit of knowing more is something each of us can do every day.

Mastering the Art of Asking: A Practical Guide

Breaking free from assumptions takes practice. It's not something that happens once with a big aha moment. Instead, it's a mindset that you cultivate day by day, decision by decision. Overcoming the comfort of certainty means learning to challenge what you think you know, to question deeply, and to stay open to what might surprise you.

At the center of the KIND Method is the radical idea that asking is one of the most courageous acts of kindness we can practice. As Millard Fuller, founder of Habitat for Humanity, often said, "We've tried asking and not asking. Asking works better."

Here is a practical guide to help you do just that.

Recognize Your Assumptions

The first step is simple awareness. Ask yourself: *Am I relying on past experiences instead of current data? Do I assume I know how others will respond—without asking? Am I avoiding certain questions because I think I already know the answers?* Assumptions thrive in silence. Naming them is the beginning of change.

Ask Something Every Day

Exercising your "asking muscle" builds resilience against assumption. It could be as small as asking a new colleague about their background, requesting feedback, or simply asking for help. The point is to get more comfortable with the discomfort of not knowing and to lean into the humility that curiosity requires.

Seek Diverse Perspectives

Don't just consult your usual circle. Bring in different voices and backgrounds, especially those that challenge your thinking. Are your media choices, routines, or relationships reinforcing the same ideas over and over? Try intentionally reading, watching, or listening to content that doesn't align with your current views. Growth doesn't come from constant agreement; it comes from stretching.

Look for Real Data, Not Just Opinions

Before making a decision, ask: *Have I looked at actual numbers, trends, or direct feedback? Have I considered other people's lived experiences, not just surface-level impressions?* Whether you're navigating change in your personal life, your community, or your organization, seek out those who've been there. Ask what worked for them and what didn't.

Create Safe Spaces for Dialogue
If you're a leader, be intentional about how your team communicates. Do your meetings invite input from everyone, or do they default to the loudest voices? Are psychological safety and listening encouraged? Making space for quiet voices often reveals powerful insight that would otherwise go unheard.

Practice Active Listening
Don't just hear to reply—listen to understand. Build relationships with people who stretch you, and ask sincere, open-ended questions. As one wise friend put it, "When we listen not to debate, but to learn, we open ourselves to wisdom we would otherwise miss."

Get Comfortable with Uncertainty
Progress requires tolerance for ambiguity. Are you leaving space for open-ended questions? Are you rushing toward easy answers or sitting with complexity? Strong leaders don't always have answers, but they have the courage to explore.

Test—Don't Assume
Rather than declaring something impossible, test it. Pilot new ideas on a small scale. Create space for failure and learning. Growth mindsets rooted in curiosity and feedback outperform rigid confidence every time.

Build a Culture of Curiosity

Whether it's in your workplace, your family, or your community, cultivate environments where asking is normal, where doubt is welcome, and where no one is expected to "know it all." Regularly schedule check-ins to revisit old assumptions and update your view based on what's newly true.

Mastering the art of asking isn't about having all the answers. It's about staying open, humble, and relentlessly curious. That's where true progress begins.

THE RIPPLE EFFECT OF KNOWING MORE

As with any real, lasting transformation, the impact of committing to knowing more begins internally, but it doesn't stay there. It radiates outward, affecting our relationships, our workplaces, our communities, and eventually the world around us.

It all starts with a mindset shift. When you approach every circumstance, whether in your personal life, your work, your volunteering, or your philanthropy, with the intention to seek deeper understanding, everything changes. Knowing more becomes a way of being, not just a nice idea or an occasional practice.

Consider your workplace. Few environments have the power to either uplift or deplete us as profoundly as the places where we spend our professional lives. People either love their work or dread it, and very often, the difference isn't the work itself. It's the environment and culture. It's whether people feel seen, valued, and heard, not just as workers but as human beings.

Can practicing Outrageous Kindness, starting with a mindset of knowing more, actually change your workplace? Absolutely. We've seen it firsthand. We've seen teams that committed to breaking down the culture of assumptions perform better, raise more money, achieve bigger goals, solve harder problems, and build stronger, more resilient relationships. When leaders and team members approach each other with curiosity rather than judgment, with a willingness to ask rather than assume, real transformation happens.

But again, it starts with humility, with the understanding that no one person has all the answers. No single perspective holds every solution. By creating better dialogue, by intentionally building bridges instead of walls, by inviting others into the process, we create environments where everyone can thrive, and when that happens, change happens within us and around us.

At a personal level, the power of asking creates micro-moments of connection that build over time into something extraordinary. I remember being out of town one day, browsing in a small local shop. The shelves were filled with unique, carefully curated items—things I wouldn't find back home. By the time I reached the register, my arms were full, but when the clerk totaled everything up, the number made me pause.

Smiling, I asked, half-joking, "Is there an out-of-town discount?"

To my surprise, the clerk laughed and said, "You know what? Sure. Let's call it a visitor's welcome gift," and gave me 25 percent off.

That moment wasn't just about saving money. It was about what asking made possible. With one small, lighthearted question, I had opened the door to a warm exchange between two strangers. It became a moment of recognition and goodwill, a brief but genuine connection that shifted the energy between us. That's the true power of asking. It tells someone: *I see you, I trust you, and I believe we might share a solution, a story, or a smile.* Over time, these little moments can ripple outward into something much bigger.

That small act of asking breaks the isolation that assumptions create. It transforms transactions into relationships and turns potential judgment into genuine partnership.

At its core, *Know more* is about honoring the dignity and humanity in every person. When we know more, we love more. When we ask more, we learn more. And when we value more, we build a better, kinder world.

CHAPTER 4

I—Identify Your Impact

THERE'S A QUOTE from *The Hobbit* movie that I come back to often. Interestingly, it wasn't penned by Tolkien himself—it appears only in the film adaptation—but it captures the heart of Outrageous Kindness so beautifully. The wizard Gandalf says:

> *Some believe it is only great powers that can hold evil in check, but I have found that it is the small, everyday deeds of ordinary folk that keep the darkness at bay. Small acts of kindness and love.*

That's it. That's the heartbeat of this chapter.

When we talk about Impact, it's easy to imagine grand, sweeping gestures—the kind that make headlines or go viral. But real impact starts small. It lives in how you choose to show up in the everyday: how you treat the people around you, how you speak to yourself, how you respond to challenges. Every action sends a ripple. Every thought, every word, every decision carries energy into the world.

Put simply, big impact begins with small deeds.

This truth echoes the concept of the butterfly effect, first proposed by meteorologist Edward Lorenz in 1972, the idea that something as delicate as the flap of a butterfly's wings can set off a chain reaction that leads to a tornado on the other side of the world.[9] Whether or not you're into chaos theory, it's a powerful metaphor. Small changes, made consistently and with intention, can shape outcomes we might never predict. That's the essence of Outrageous Kindness: the quiet faith that love in motion will go farther than we can see.

Many people never make those small changes because they don't know what difference their kindness will make. When you don't have a clear sense of impact, the little things can feel like drops in a bucket with no bottom. Clarity of purpose changes that. When you understand the bigger story you're helping to write, it becomes easier and more joyful to take meaningful action in the present.

Not long ago, Susan and I had dinner with a couple. They're both warm, successful, and generous people. The man was a potential business partner, but the real impact of that evening came in the conversation we shared. Like many people who learn what we do, they began opening up about the causes they care about and the challenges they face in making a difference.

The woman spoke passionately about a small, mission-driven nonprofit she supports in Kenya. Each year, she works tirelessly to raise funds. But lately, she admitted, it's been getting harder. "I'm going back to the same group of friends year after year," she said. "They give, but I think it's mostly out of loyalty now, not passion."

Then she asked, almost tentatively, "What do you think I should do?"

Instead of jumping in with a solution, I asked her a question of my own: "How much money do you need to raise over the next five years?"

There was a pause. Then her husband looked up, intrigued. "That's a great question," he said. "But why five years?"

I explained that most of us are so focused on the immediate—this month, this quarter—that we forget how uninspiring urgency can be on its own. What truly moves people isn't pressure. It's vision. It's the invitation to be part of something bigger than themselves.

As the couple began to picture what five years of impact could look like, something changed. They stopped thinking about short-term fundraising and started dreaming about infrastructure. What if they could build a school? Install clean water systems? Support an entire village?

Suddenly, the question wasn't "How do we raise more money this year?" It was "How do we transform lives for generations?"

That's the power of an Outrageous Goal.

CALLED BEYOND OUR LIMITS

These goals aren't just about ambition. They're about vision—bold, stretch, purpose-driven goals that call us beyond our limits. They challenge what we think is possible and demand that we grow into who we were meant to be.

For organizations, entrepreneurs, or anyone called to do meaningful work, an Outrageous Goal reframes everything. It elevates your thinking. It accelerates your results. And when paired with Outrageous Kindness, the impact doesn't just multiply—it transcends.

This isn't just about dreaming big. It's about *acting* big. It's about believing deeply in what's possible when we combine faith, love, collaboration, and persistence. Will we always hit every target? No. But when we commit fully and celebrate the progress along the way, we become vessels of something far more powerful than personal success: We become builders of legacy.

Create a vision so compelling that others can see themselves in it, and never forget—how you live in the small moments is the most powerful lever you'll ever have.

DEFINING IMPACT

When we talk about Impact in the context of Outrageous Kindness, we're really talking about something that lives on two levels—personal and collective. It's not just about making large-scale changes. It's about showing up in a way that truly matters, day after day, moment by moment.

On a personal level, impact begins with knowing yourself and understanding what brings you joy and moves your heart. What matters most to you? This might be something as simple as your love for animals. Maybe you feel fulfilled when you move a turtle off the road or volunteer with a rescue shelter. That's Impact. It doesn't have to be grand to be meaningful. What's important is that it comes from a place of love and purpose.

I often think about my late husband when he was seriously ill. His health was failing, his energy was limited, and his world had grown very small, yet each day he set a goal for himself to make someone smile. That was his impact. It was what he could do, and having a goal and reaching it mattered to him and others. I had countless caregivers, nurses, and others tell me how much they looked forward to spending time with him because he brightened their days.

Impact isn't about scope—it's about *intention*. It's about how we show up, even in the smallest of ways. When we're going through times of grief, pain, or uncertainty, staying connected to our own sense of purpose can anchor us by reminding us that our effort and our kindness still have power.

On a broader scale, in terms of teams and organizations, Impact means being deeply rooted in your mission and remaining connected to your *why*. That may sound obvious, but in practice, it's incredibly easy to drift. In nonprofit circles, we call this "mission creep."

Here's how it usually happens. You start with a clear goal. For example, improving access to quality education for kids in a specific neighborhood. But then a grant opportunity comes along to fund after-school sports. The money is helpful, so you accept it. Before long, you're in the sports programming business, but reading and math scores still haven't improved. The original problem you set out to solve is still there because the mission lost its focus.

This drift happens in businesses too. A team launches with energy and purpose, but without a clear, shared understanding of what success looks like, team members start operating in silos. Leaders try to motivate through bonuses or perks, hoping to boost enthusiasm, but recognition without purpose doesn't fuel performance for long.

What *does* fuel performance is a bold, shared goal. In my experience, the most effective and fulfilled teams are the ones that can answer two key questions:

1. What are we here to do?
2. What does success look like?

Whether you're building a company, leading a nonprofit, or parenting a family, clarity of purpose and measurable impact are what inspire and unite people. Not some "Star of the Month" badge, but the vision of what we're building together.

Think about any high-performing sports team. They aren't just playing for fun—they're playing to win. Their goal is to make it to the championships, and that collective ambition bonds people and generates momentum. When things get hard—and they always do—it keeps them grounded.

For the last four summers, I've witnessed the remarkable power of a shared goal to unite high-achieving young people. They endure fourteen-to-sixteen-hour days of intense work, mostly outdoors, with long bus rides, limited personal time, and a constant demand for teamwork. All of it builds toward a performance that lasts just eight minutes. As a proud Drum Corps International mom with a front-row seat to their commitment and discipline, I walk away from every rehearsal and show reflecting on the deep impact this experience has on the group.[10] It's a masterclass in self-sacrifice, resilience, collaboration, celebration, and growth. If you ever have the chance to hire someone who has spent their summer in drum corps, take it. You'll be impressed.

Define your impact, personally and collectively. Name it and aim for it. Let it be the compass that guides you and keeps you pointed in the right direction.

THE FEAR THAT KEEPS US SMALL

If we can't always achieve our Outrageous Goals, why aim for them in the first place?

Because the very act of aiming high is life-changing.

Nonprofit organizations are often on the front lines of solving some of the world's most pressing problems, usually with limited resources. In my work, I've led countless assessments for well-known nonprofits to determine whether they're "ready" to launch major fundraising campaigns to scale their impact.

Here's what I've learned: Almost no one is ever fully ready before they begin.

You rarely get the perfect plan, the perfect moment, or the perfect team in place ahead of time. Most of the time, we're "riding the bike while we build it." And that's OK.

Why? Because Outrageous Goals demand urgency, and in that urgency, we find clarity. They force us to admit that "business as usual" is no longer enough. We stop waiting for flawless conditions and start mapping out tangible, short-term actions that lead us forward. I've seen this approach work again and again, helping teams raise billions of dollars for causes that truly matter.

But what happens when that mindset doesn't come easily? What can we do when perfectionism or self-doubt gets in the way? It's the Self One, the "teller," as described by Gallwey, as we mentioned earlier.

I've wrestled with it myself. There's a quiet force that holds more power over our lives than we often admit. It doesn't show up as a shout but as a whisper. It doesn't slam doors—it hesitates. It says, "Not yet." It says, "Maybe later." That force is fear.

Fear convinces us that we need to have everything figured out before we begin. That we need more qualifications, more clarity, more control. It tells us the timing has to be perfect, or worse, that *we* have to be perfect. And until then, we wait.

I've lived this. I've heard the voice in my head that says, "You're not ready," or "You're not enough," or "Who do you think you are?" I've let it stop me in my tracks more than once.

I am grateful for the wise voices in my life who gently remind me that perfection isn't the goal. Starting is.

This is especially important when it comes to kindness. We so often fall into the trap of thinking our impact has to be big, impressive, or polished to matter, but that's simply not true. You can begin right now, with what you have, right where you are.

Fear says, "Wait until you're ready." "What if you fail?" "What if people laugh?" And so we shrink back. We lower the bar. We scale back our dreams and goals and settle for safe and small when what the world desperately needs is bold and loving.

Fear wears many faces. There's the fear of failure, of course, but there's also fear of the unknown. There's fear of vulnerability, fear of doing it wrong, and, yes, even fear of what might happen if we actually succeed.

Any of these fears can block the very things we're called to do. They keep us from listening deeply, from reaching out to those we don't understand, and sometimes even from engaging with people just like us because we fear rejection or discomfort.

In today's world, fear is often weaponized. It's used to divide, to distract, to dehumanize, but Outrageous Kindness is the antidote. It invites us to lean in with open hearts, to lead with love even when we're unsure, even when the outcome isn't guaranteed.

I think of a story from the book of Exodus in the Bible, where a man named Moses is called by God to lead a group of people out of slavery in Egypt. At first, he's overwhelmed with fear. He doesn't feel qualified or capable, and he pleads to be excused from the task. But ultimately, he chooses to trust the calling, even though he lacks confidence. Through that act of obedience, he begins to grow into the courageous leader he was meant to become.

That's what courage really is—not the absence of fear but action in the face of it.

Young people especially need to hear this. You don't need every tool in the toolbox to make a difference. You already have creative power. You have digital power. You have relational and emotional power. But fear will try to convince you that you don't.

Even writing this book came with its own fears. It had to be pristine from the first paragraph. I have seen that writing doesn't work that way. Neither does life.

In early 2025, I attended a screenwriting panel at the Oxford Film Festival, an organization I help lead. The author and now filmmaker Michael Farris Smith shared the opening scene of his short film *Chasing Rabbits*. In it, a woman awakens in her home to find it vandalized and covered in graffiti. Someone in the audience asked, "Did you outline your script, and did you already know where the story was going when you wrote that?"

He smiled. "No. I had no idea." He further explained that he likes to create characters, put them in circumstances, and see what happens.

That answer stunned me. How could you start without knowing the ending?

But of course, that's exactly how the creative process works. That's how *life* works. We start, not because we know where it's going, but because something inside us says it's time. Sometimes, the first step is taken in faith, into the unknown.

If we let fear stop us, we'll never take that step. So don't wait. Don't hold your kindness hostage to your doubts. Don't shrink your goals because the path isn't clear yet. Begin anyway. Trust that the vision will evolve. Trust that the road will rise to meet your courage.

LIVING A LIFE OF IMPACT ONE MOMENT AT A TIME

You don't have to wait for the "right" moment to create an impact, nor do you need to create a polished five-year plan or launch a nonprofit with your name on the door. You can create an impact simply by how you show up in ordinary life—in your laughter, your heartbreak, your anger, and your joy.

When people ask me how they can begin to identify and grow their impact, and how they can stay committed to it for the long haul, I start with a few simple questions:

- *When was the last time you cried?* Not from physical pain, but because something *moved* you. Because your heart broke a little at the state of the world, or for someone else's suffering. That kind of sorrow reveals what matters most to you. It points to the causes, the stories, and the people that stir your soul.
- *When was the last time you laughed—really laughed?* What brought you joy? Did a piece of music stir something deep within you? Did a child's curiosity make you smile? Did a conversation leave you feeling lighter, more hopeful, more alive? These are not trivial emotions. They are clues. If something brings you joy, maybe part of your impact is sharing that joy with others. Maybe your purpose is tucked inside that moment.
- *What makes you angry?* What injustice lights a fire inside you? What issue makes your stomach turn or your fists clench? That, too, is a compass. Our anger, when harnessed with compassion, can point us toward our most powerful work. It reflects the values we hold and the wrongs we feel called to help make right.
- *Who or what has inspired you?* Is there a movie, book, performance, or other artwork that has motivated you in a profound way? Is there another person who has impacted you in a way that you want to pay forward?

In regard to that last question, a colleague of mine shared an amazing story about her son. One day, while walking across his college campus, her son was wearing a hoodie with the logo of his Ohio high school. A man driving by in a golf cart noticed and stopped him. He inquired about the high school logo.

As it turned out, the man had graduated from the very same high school *and* the same college that this young man was now attending. The man also happened to be a successful CEO and entrepreneur. What started as a chance encounter turned into a two-hour conversation about life, school, and ambition. Before they parted ways, the CEO offered to stay in touch and help the young man learn more about business if he was interested.

Over the next few months, they exchanged emails and phone calls. Then, during spring break, the CEO invited the student to shadow him at his company, giving him a front-row seat to real-world business leadership. The young man followed him through meetings, observed how decisions were made, and got a glimpse into both the big-picture strategy and the daily details that keep a business running. By the end of the week, the CEO extended an offer for a summer internship.

Overwhelmed with gratitude, the student finally asked, "This is so generous. Why are you doing this?"

"Two reasons," the CEO replied. "First, when I was your age— and not doing particularly well in school—someone gave me the same kind of opportunity, and it changed my life. Second, I see potential in you."

This is how kindness moves. Sometimes, it's one person stopping a stranger to say, "I see you, and I'd like to help."

There's one more lens that reveals a great deal about the impact you're already making, whether we realize it or not: How are you spending your time and money? Nothing exposes our values more clearly than where we invest our two most limited resources. An often-quoted phrase is "time is the ultimate equalizer." Meaning no one—no billionaire, no guru, no world leader—gets more than twenty-four hours in a day, and how we use those hours says more about our priorities than any mission statement ever could.

I'll be honest: I scroll. I get caught in the rabbit holes of social media like anyone else, but lately, I've become more intentional. Instead of simply doom-scrolling, I've started to seek out and share reels that reflect the values of Outrageous Kindness. The more I share those kinds of reels, the more of them I *see*. The algorithm begins to change.

Now, instead of being fed ads for wrinkle creams or dating over fifty or yet another promise to lose ten pounds (oops, I guess you know a little more about me now), I'm seeing videos of kindness. People helping people. People celebrating small wins. People reminding each other what really matters. In other words, the more I focus on what matters most to me, the more of it shows up.

HONORING THE QUIET SEASONS OF IMPACT

I want to speak directly here to those of you in the "sandwich generation," who are juggling kids and aging parents, maybe even grandkids, and a demanding career. If you're in a season of caregiving, know this: You are *already* making an impact.

If this isn't the season to start a bold new venture or launch a passion project, that's OK. You are making a difference. Maybe the way you create impact right now is by playing music for your parents in the evenings. Maybe it's helping your grandchild discover their love of the piano. Maybe it's as simple as offering a word of encouragement, a smile, or a warm meal. And I hope it's also in the way in which you speak to yourself about what you're doing.

Someone said to me recently that they admired Susan and me for launching a new business "at our ages." I laughed, more at the candor than the comment, but decided to lean into the moment. Seeking to *Know more*, I asked what they meant.

"Well," they said, "there's so much being written these days about how ageism and sexism can make older women almost invisible at work. People start thinking more about safety nets than taking on new risks."

I understood where they were coming from, but I also knew my own story. When my husband died and our son was just fourteen, I had the itch to launch something new, to chase the spark of a fresh adventure. But we were in the middle of a global pandemic. My husband's long illness had been a storm we'd weathered as a family, and now my deepest desire was to create a season of stability for my son and for myself.

So, I waited. I hadn't lost the fire, but I knew the most important impact I could have in that season was showing up. I stayed in the house filled with memories. I turned down work travel, reduced video calls, and created space. The dreams and ideas didn't go away. They simmered. And in that space, I was given the sacred gift of watching my son grow.

So now is *exactly* the right time. The culture may carry assumptions about what women "should" or "shouldn't" do at a certain age, but I know purpose doesn't follow a timeline, and it certainly doesn't fade with age.

If you're in this "sandwich" season of life, between caring for others, navigating loss, or reimagining your future, please give yourself grace. Purpose doesn't always show up as a business plan or a global movement. Sometimes, it's a quiet act of love done with great care. Choose joy, trust the timing, and know there is deep honor in the unseen, sacred work you are doing right now.

THE POWER OF PURPOSEFUL GIVING

As I mentioned, how you spend your financial resources is one of the greatest indicators of your values. So, one of the most significant ways we can make an impact is through our giving. Giving isn't just good for the world—it's good for *you*. When done purposefully and consistently, giving roots us in our values, affirms our identity, and connects us with others in deeply meaningful ways.

I was lucky to learn this early in my professional life from a man named Dr. Doug Lawson. Back in the 1990s, Dr. Lawson was considered a pioneer in the field of philanthropy. He was an innovative fundraising mind who worked closely with major institutions and high-net-worth individuals to help align their giving with their deepest values.

Doug wrote a book called *Give to Live*, and its simple but profound message was "when we give, we come alive." Whether it's our money, our time, our talent, or even our social connections, giving feeds us. It builds our sense of purpose, our resilience, and even our joy.[11]

This idea isn't just a theory. Modern research echoes what Doug's work revealed decades ago. Giving has measurable mental, emotional, and even physical benefits. It lifts our moods, combats isolation, and gives our days direction. It also grounds us in something larger than ourselves.[12]

Today, I'm working with a wonderful author named Dale Alexander, who's written a book for young people about money titled *"The Talk" (About Money): A Young Adult's Guide to the One*

Decision That Changes Everything.[13] His premise is that if you learn to live on less than you earn from your very first paycheck, you'll be richer in every way. Dale teaches a principle I was raised on myself: Give away 10 percent of what you make *always*. Whether you give to your church, your school, a local charity, or a cause close to your heart, that giving creates freedom, not scarcity.

When we give from what we have, no matter how little, we're making a statement to ourselves: "I have enough to share." Some of the most generous people I've ever met don't have much in terms of financial resources, but what they *do* have, they give freely. They are generous with their time, their presence, their skills, and, yes, their kindness. In doing so, they participate in the healing of their communities and the nourishing of their own souls.

There's also a practical side to generosity that doesn't get talked about enough. It builds what I call *social capital*. Financial capital is important—that includes your income, your savings, your investments—but social capital is just as important. That includes your relationships, your community, and the people you can turn to when life throws you a curveball.

For example, a few days ago, I was talking to a friend who owns a large construction company. One of his workers had stepped on a nail and was experiencing worsening pain in his leg. It quickly became clear the man had never had a tetanus shot, and worse, he wasn't part of the formal health-care system. Frankly, he feared it. He just didn't know where to turn.

My friend had gotten to know a local emergency room doctor through their shared involvement in supporting an arts organization. This relationship was invaluable at the moment. To help, my friend picked up the phone and called his doctor friend, who arranged for the worker to come to the side entrance of the hospital—no paperwork required, no questions asked. He got his shot, his leg was treated, and the crisis was averted.

That's social capital in action. It's the kind of impact you can't always measure. When you participate in philanthropy in any way, you become part of a network of people who care. And people who care tend to be generous not just with their money but with their *help*. They introduce you to others. They show up for you when life gets hard. They open doors and lend wisdom. And you become that kind of person for others, too.

This is why having a philanthropic purpose matters. It changes you, expands your network, and strengthens your emotional core. It gives you something solid to stand on when everything else feels uncertain.

Whether you're donating, volunteering, mentoring, introducing people, or simply offering a kind word, you are participating in something much bigger than yourself. You are investing in your values, and you are building a legacy of kindness that money alone could never buy.

WHY KINDNESS IS GOOD FOR BUSINESS TOO

Let's clear up a common misconception. When people hear about *Outrageous Kindness* or the *KIND Method*, they sometimes assume it's only for those who want to live a philanthropic lifestyle, maybe volunteering in soup kitchens or signing up for a year with AmeriCorps. However, that's not the whole story, not even close. You don't have to sell everything you own or abandon your career to live a life of deep impact. In fact, one of the most powerful ways you can make a difference in the world is by building a wildly successful, ethical, people-first business. That's right. *Success itself can be an act of kindness.*

Consider what it means to create a company that not only generates profit, but does so while taking exceptional care of its employees. A company that delivers quality products in sustainable, thoughtful ways, that supports families, uplifts communities, and builds something that lasts.

That is Impact. Creating real, meaningful jobs is one of the most generous things you can do. It gives people agency. It gives them purpose. It helps them discover their own gifts and contribute in ways that make the world better.

When FedEx founder Fred Smith passed away in June 2025, tributes poured in, not just for his revolutionary business acumen, but for the genuine kindness he showed the community he called home. As one Memphis official remarked, "Memphis has lost its most important citizen." It's a fitting tribute to a leader whose generosity reached far beyond the boardroom.

Fred Smith's commitment to building FedEx in Memphis added to the community's economic stability and created lifelong jobs for hundreds of people. Smith's approach to leadership at FedEx was rooted in empathy and service. During the early days of the COVID-19 pandemic, for example, he used his company's logistical power to deliver surgical masks and vaccines when they were desperately needed. Smith's swift actions saved lives and showed what can happen when business leadership doubles as an act of kindness.

Smith rarely sought recognition for his donations to institutions like the Marine Corps Scholarship Foundation, the Memphis Zoo, or local universities. When asked why he gave, he offered a humble rationale: "If you've done well in this country, it's pretty churlish for you not to at least be willing to give a pretty good portion of that back to the public interest."[14]

Fred Smith's life and leadership remind us that kindness, at its best, can transform not only a company or a city, but the hearts of everyone touched by it.

When you make money ethically, your success lifts others up with you. You're not taking from the world; you're contributing to it. So, let's stop pretending that business and kindness are at odds. They're not. In fact, kindness is a business advantage. The companies that win today are the ones that treat people like people—not just numbers. They have strong cultures and lead with empathy.

In fact, 72 percent of Millennials and Gen Z say they prioritize purpose over salary when choosing a job, and 64 percent of US consumers make purchasing decisions based on a company's social values. Purpose isn't just a feel-good idea—it's a growth strategy.[15]

This is why I say the KIND Method is a strategic advantage for founders, leaders, and changemakers. It's how you build cultures that last while retaining talent and driving innovation. And that's how you create brands that people love and trust.

So if you're someone with big dreams, someone who wants to grow a business, make a living, and do good all at once—this is your permission slip. You can and you *should*. Success and kindness are not mutually exclusive. On the contrary, when done right, they become partners. The more you grow, the more good you can do, not in spite of your ambition but *because* of it.

Go build the thing. Dream big. Make money. Change lives. Just do it with kindness at the core. That's how we change the world.

LONG-TERM VISION AND SHORT-TERM ACTION

Outrageous Goals can take years, even decades, to fully realize. They're not quick wins. They are your North Star, your long game, the dream that gives meaning to the mundane and direction to the daily. These are the goals that shape how you live, what you stand for, and how you want to serve. They help define who you're becoming.

But as powerful as long-term vision is, it doesn't move on its own. You need momentum, and that requires short-term goals. These are the stepping stones—the daily, weekly, even monthly wins that build confidence and keep the dream alive. They're smaller in scale but no less sacred. In fact, they're what makes the big stuff possible. They teach us how to course-correct, how to pivot with grace, and how to stay in motion even when the path is unclear.

My very first job interview in college was with a big Fortune 500 company. The interviewer asked me, "Where do you see yourself in ten years?"

I answered, with all the boldness of a young woman full of hope and fire, "I will be the CEO of an innovative company. I want to lead something that makes a difference."

He didn't laugh—not exactly—but I'll never forget his response: "I don't see that happening."

In hindsight, I'm sure I had no real idea what it took to be a CEO, but I already had a vision. I knew I wanted to lead with purpose. I knew I wanted to use my gifts to make the world better. I wasn't interested in small dreams, even if I didn't yet know the map to get there.

That moment planted a seed. It didn't discourage me. It clarified it to me. My mother helped too.

JUST GET A JOB

My mother had a very practical way of viewing things and a beautiful ability to cut through complex thoughts with simple, everyday wisdom. Whenever I would share my struggles about how to reach my ultimate career goals, she would listen—somewhat patiently—and then offer, "Just get a job."

Her motherly advice would remind me:

- Want to be a CEO? First, you have to get a job.
- Want to make the world more beautiful? Make your bed.
- Want people to be nicer? Stop complaining.

In other words, you have to start where you are, not where you want to end up. Your impact doesn't begin someday. It starts now, in how you do what's right in front of you.

I go back to that phrase regularly. Even writing this book, when I was faced with fear about whether anyone would read it, I remembered to "get a job." In this case, that meant just start writing.

When defining the broader impact you want to make in life, starting is essential for these reasons and more:

1. *Every experience is a classroom.* By showing up and doing the work, you learn more about yourself, refine your goals, and sharpen your talents.
2. *You build social capital and relationship wisdom.* Working with others teaches patience, communication, and the value of collaboration and builds connection.
3. *Discipline is developed through consistency.* Showing up daily, especially when it's hard, builds the muscle that will carry you through bigger challenges later.
4. *Momentum matters.* Getting started creates movement, and movement creates confidence. I cannot help but think of all the times my single friends talk about dating karma (i.e., you meet more people if you start dating than if you do not).

5. *You grow into your purpose.* Often, you don't find your calling and then act—you act, and in doing so, you find your calling.

This idea also echoes Marcus Buckingham's strength-based matrix, which suggests that your true strengths lie not just in what you're good at but in what strengthens you, what energizes and excites you, even if it requires effort. But you can't discover that from the sidelines. You "just get a job," and in the doing, you start to notice what lights you up and what drains you. The work becomes a mirror revealing not only your competence but your joy. That's how daily tasks align with a deeper sense of purpose.[16]

Reflection Exercise: Your Impact Is Right in Front of You

OBJECTIVE

To help you recognize where you can begin now and where your energy is pointing you.

Step 1: Take Inventory

List three things you're currently responsible for—whether at work, home, or in your community. These don't have to be glamorous or "big." They can be as ordinary as doing dishes, leading a meeting, or showing up on time.

1. _____

2. _____

3. _____

Step 2: Observe Your Energy

Next to each one, write whether it:

- *Strengthens* you (energizes, excites, or brings fulfillment)
- *Neutralizes* you (neither drains nor energizes)
- *Drains* you (leaves you exhausted, frustrated, or disengaged)

Here is my example:

1. Leading workshops that inspire people to take action and make a difference—*Strengthens me.*
2. Any form of paperwork or filling out of forms—*Drains me.*
3. Managing emails—*Neutral.*

Step 3: Reflect

Answer these prompts:

- What surprised you about what strengthens or drains you?
- Is there one task that drains you but you do well? What might that tell you?
- Could the principle of asking for something (from the "Know More" chapter) help you focus more

on your strengths and lean into the strengths
of others?

- What's one way you can bring more of what
  strengthens you into your week—even in
  small ways?

Step 4: Just Get a Job
Now, pick **one small thing you can do this week**
to move in the direction of your goals. Think action
over perfection.

This week, I will: _____

With these reflections in mind, remember this: Outrageous Goals
aren't for the faint of heart. Landing a job is just the beginning. To
keep going—to keep growing—you'll need courage, adaptability,
and a deep willingness to learn. Learn from your missteps. Learn
from the wisdom of others. Learn from the quiet, ordinary steps
that shape extraordinary outcomes.

As you move from "just getting a job" to chasing something
bigger, keep this in mind: Setting the goal is one thing, but *living
into it* is where the transformation happens. Remember to:

- *Break it down.* Take your bold vision and divide it into clear,
  tangible milestones. Clarity fuels momentum.
- *Just begin.* Don't wait for perfect timing. Take the first
  step—small or large—and let progress reveal the path.
- *Act like the person you're becoming.* Show up as if you're
  already living that next chapter.

- *Let failure teach you.* Don't avoid it—expect it. Let it shape you, not stop you.
- *Ask for help.* Share your vision. Listen with humility. Leadership grows in community, not isolation.
- *Stay grounded in purpose.* The right goal will stretch you *and* serve something beyond you.

Now take a breath and ask yourself:

- What am I working toward right now?
- Is it pulling me forward or just helping me stand still?

If it's not stretching you, maybe it's time to go bolder. Make it Outrageous. And as you pursue it, let kindness lead the way. Encourage others without condition. Bring hope, honesty, and wholeness to every space you enter, just by being fully you.

Because when boldness and kindness walk hand in hand, there's no limit to the impact you can make.

CHAPTER 5

N—Navigate

I T STARTED LIKE any other travel day. The gate agent called for passengers who needed extra time or assistance, and a few people made their way toward the plane. The ticket scanner beeped, bags wheeled behind the first passengers, as they disappeared down the jet bridge.

However, a few minutes later, I saw them returning, confused. Something wasn't right. Then, a buzz from my phone: "Your flight has been delayed." Strange. They had already started boarding. Why was the flight delayed *now*?

The gate agent picked up the microphone. "We're missing a pilot," she said, as if she were announcing a minor delay due to weather.

After three decades of business travel, I've learned that delays are rarely what they seem on the surface. As we said in a previous chapter, if you want to make a smart decision, you have to get curious. You have to *ask* and seek more information. So I approached the gate agent gently and asked, "Is the pilot flying in on another flight?"

"No," she replied. "He's driving in. Should be here by seven forty-five."

Now, this was Atlanta, which is famous for traffic and unpredictable commutes. A seven-forty-five arrival could easily turn into eighty thirty or nine. That's a lot of sitting, waiting, and hoping, so I started looking at my options. I researched other flights and found one leaving around the same time the pilot was expected to arrive. It was a bit of a gamble, but something about it felt better than waiting around with growing uncertainty.

After thinking it over, I gave up my seat and switched flights. The new gate was across the terminal. I made my way there, hopeful, but halfway through the journey, my phone buzzed again: "New flight delayed."

I stopped right there in the middle of the terminal.

Now what?

Do I keep walking toward a new flight with an unknown issue? Or do I turn around and go back to the original flight with a familiar problem, but likely a longer wait and less promising outcome?

I stood there, stuck, torn between what I *knew* and what I *hoped*. And that's when it hit me: *This is exactly the decision I've been avoiding in my work.*

For three days, I had been spinning my wheels, paralyzed by a choice. On the one hand, I was being offered a guaranteed project with a paycheck that felt safe and structured but deeply unsatisfying. It was the "original flight" of my business strategy—predictable but unlikely to take me where I really wanted to go. On the other hand, I had an alternative that offered a new direction with more upside, more momentum, but more unknowns. I couldn't yet see every piece, I didn't have a map, but I had a sense. A tug and a passion.

I kept walking to the new flight. When I reached the gate, I learned the delay was minor, just a patch of weather that the plane needed to route around. Within minutes, we were boarding, and I ended up arriving at my destination earlier than I would have if I had stayed put.

This is what it means to Navigate. It's not about knowing everything. It's about responding wisely when the path changes. It's about listening to your inner wisdom, your instinct, your sense of what's aligned and what's calling you forward.

That means being willing to pause midstride and ask, *Is this still the right flight?*

Outrageous Kindness asks us to extend that grace to ourselves by allowing uncertainty to inform us but not define us. We must accept that we'll never have all the data and then walk forward anyway with courage, humility, and curiosity.

When we learn to Navigate—not with fear, but with faith—we discover that delays can lead to clarity, detours can bring revelation, and the real destination might not be the gate we first walked toward but the one we had the heart to find. Navigate is not just choosing the obvious option. It's about pausing, gathering insight, asking questions, and making clear, informed decisions, even when uncertainty is involved.

In the KIND Method, Navigate means having the courage and clarity to move forward when the road forks. Sometimes, moving forward is exactly what gets you there faster.

NAVIGATING THE UNEXPECTED WITH KINDNESS

When I talk to groups about what it means to navigate, I often begin with a simple question:

When was the last time your day went exactly the way you thought it would?

The room usually fills with knowing laughter or soft groans because the truth is things *never* go exactly as planned, not 99.9 percent of the time, especially if you're someone who is raising children, caring for aging parents, building a business, or in any way actively trying to create positive change in the world. If you're chasing Outrageous Goals or committing yourself to bold kindness, disruption is a given. You can't even go to the grocery store without something unexpected happening. Maybe someone cuts you off in traffic, the checkout line freezes up, or they're out of the one ingredient you need.

For that reason, and a laundry list of others, I don't particularly like going to the grocery store. When the pandemic hit and grocery delivery services became widespread, I was first in line and never looked back. However, the point remains: Even the smallest daily tasks are often thrown off-course. That's just how the world works now, if it ever worked any other way.

In fact, many of the global humanitarian organizations I've worked with describe the world as being in a state of "perma-crisis." It used to be that a natural disaster would occur, or a conflict would erupt, and there would be a clear beginning, middle, and end. The world would rally, rebuild, and recover. But now, it seems constant. One crisis folds into the next. A new war breaks out before another ends. The pace of disruption is relentless.

When you're working in international aid, trying to accomplish something outrageous like making sure every child on the planet has access to clean water, that kind of instability demands constant adaptation. I've seen organizations wrestle with things like, *What happens when the wells we've dug are destroyed every few months by armed factions?* or *How do we pivot when the US government unexpectedly changes foreign aid rules, sending our entire funding model into a tailspin overnight?*

These are not minor obstacles. These are mission-threatening challenges, and yet the work must go on. If you believe in your purpose, you *must* learn to Navigate.

The same is true in business, leadership, and life. Whether you're leading a corporation, launching a nonprofit, or raising a family, the question is not *if* the plan will go sideways; it's *when*. The real test is how you respond when it does, because that's when kindness matters most. It's easy to be kind when the numbers are up and the plan is working, but what happens when tariffs go up and margins go down? When a storm derails your supply chain? When your star employee resigns unexpectedly?

Do you still treat people with dignity? Do you still speak with patience? Do you still operate from your values, even when your ROI takes a hit?

Navigate is about choosing to stay rooted in kindness *despite* disruption. It's about maintaining clarity and grace when the world throws you into uncertainty, whether it's a broken cash register or a major source of funding evaporates. So let this be a gentle reminder: You need a way to navigate not just the logistics of life but the emotional turbulence that comes with unpredictability. When your plan changes—and it *will*—the only thing that can keep you grounded is your commitment to how you want to show up, no matter what.

WORST-CASE-SCENARIO PLANNING

Most people don't struggle to be kind when life is calm and controlled. The real test that determines whether kindness is a value or just a convenience comes when things don't go as planned. That's where many of us fall short. Think about it. You're on a packed flight. There's a baby screaming behind you. Your seat keeps getting kicked. You're tired. You're frustrated. *That* is a moment of truth. Will you lean into grace and patience or let discomfort harden you?

Kindness in those moments doesn't come instinctively. It must be intentional, and that's where the *skill* of navigation comes in. Learning to navigate isn't just about making good decisions or staying calm. It's about choosing to stay anchored in your values, especially when disruption tries to knock you off course.

The question to ask yourself is, *How do I respond to change in a way that honors who I want to be?*

Let me give you an example. During the COVID-19 pandemic, many schools were scrambling as they pivoted to online learning and tried to react to a flood of uncertainty. However, there was one school I worked with that responded differently. Instead of letting the chaos redefine them, they used that moment to reaffirm who they were. They reexamined their core values and asked themselves what it really meant to educate a child, especially in a time of crisis. And then, courageously, they engaged their entire community in that conversation.

They didn't use change as a reason to compromise. Instead, they used it as a chance to connect more deeply with their mission. As the pandemic slowly came to an end, the school emerged with a bold strategic plan for the future that saw increased enrollment and raised more than $100 million for new programs and facilities that were aligned with the affirmations received when they engaged their families. That's what navigating with kindness looks like in practice.

It's not always about pivoting to something new. Sometimes, it's about rooting more deeply in what matters most. Other times, the path is less clear. When you're building something new, the risks feel bigger. Maybe there's a financial risk, or maybe there's emotional vulnerability in the looming possibility of failure. In those seasons, I've learned to do something often called *worst-case scenario planning.*

It's simple but powerful. I ask myself, *What's the worst that could happen? What if the venture flops? What if there's no income for a year? What if the whole thing crumbles?*

And then I ask, *Even in that scenario, how do I stay kind? How do I remain connected to my core values and who I want to be in the world?*

This kind of planning is about creating psychological safety for your brain. When we take fear off the throne, we can think more clearly, respond more compassionately, and stay aligned with our purpose.

No one likes to admit it, but we're not really in control. We like to think we are. We organize our calendars, build our businesses, structure our families, and plan out every hour of the day as if life will follow our lead, but it rarely does.

That's when things get hard, and people stop being kind. Why does this happen? Because disruption triggers a primal fear in us, a fear of not being in control.

Change, especially unexpected change, stirs our deepest discomfort. It reminds us that we don't run the universe. We don't have the final say, and unless we've prepared ourselves to face that reality with resilience, we'll default to frustration instead of kindness.

That's why I embrace and recommend worst-case scenario planning. I know it sounds a little intense, but it's powerful. Worst-case scenario planning helps you identify your fears before they show up. It lets you mentally walk through the disruptions that could derail you and practice how you'll stay grounded in your values when they come.

It's not about being pessimistic. It's about being prepared.

Even the most sophisticated economic models and government forecasts can't predict every disruption. No one saw Tampa getting hit by two hurricanes in one month in 2024. No one could have guessed one of those storms would travel up the East Coast and slam into the mountains of North Carolina, flooding towns, destroying roads and parks, closing schools, and leaving communities in crisis for months. But that's what happened.

Hurricane Helene devastated many towns in Western North Carolina, including Banner Elk, where Susan lives.

Late September is usually a magical time in the mountains—locals preparing for leaf peepers, fall festivals, and crisp autumn weather. Like many mountain towns, Banner Elk's economy depends on tourism: fall foliage, winter skiing, and summer escapes. No one imagined Helene would gain such terrifying strength as it moved inland, but it did, triggering over 1,600 landslides, wiping out power grids, rupturing water systems, and flattening entire communities. Lives were lost, many from families who had called those mountains home for generations.

It could have been the end of the story, but it wasn't. Instead of retreating or complaining, the people—alumni, students, staff, neighbors—rallied. They grabbed whatever tools they had and got to work. Together, they cleaned up and rebuilt. They leaned on each other, and in the process, they turned something broken into something beautiful. That's what it means to navigate change with kindness.

In the hours, days, weeks, and months that followed, the people of Banner Elk showed their true colors. Heroes emerged. Neighbors united. They got *Mountain Strong*.

There are countless stories of humanity at its best from this small but mighty community. Too many to tell, but one that Susan shared stayed with me because it reflects all four pillars of the KIND Method.

Rick Owen is the Town Manager of Banner Elk. His wife, Nancy, serves alongside him as director of tourism. Rick is a quiet, steady leader; Nancy, a dynamo. A perfect yin and yang. After Helene struck and many—including Susan—were forced to evacuate, people craved information, not from national news outlets, but from home.

Within hours, Rick began posting updates on Facebook. These weren't just tactical updates, but detailed messages full of deep gratitude for the volunteers, and gentle but firm pleas for outsiders to stay away unless they were part of trained relief efforts. Despite his own exhaustion and heartbreak, Rick kept posting day after day.

His updates helped people *Know* what was really happening on the ground. They illustrated the *Impact* of the storm and the heroic efforts of local volunteers. They showed just how hard it would be to *Navigate* the road to recovery. And they reminded everyone how important it was to keep *Delivering* resources, support, and solutions, around the clock, from across the country.

That's what leadership looks like. That's what kindness looks like. And that's what it means to turn devastation into a movement of hope.

ASK STRATEGIC QUESTIONS

Every moment of disruption is an opportunity and an invitation to practice Outrageous Kindness, and the more we prepare ourselves to meet change with grace, the more likely we are to rise when everything else around us feels like it's falling apart.

When somebody's short with you, or rude, or when they do something that upsets you, how do you respond? Do you stay calm? Do you pause and check your assumptions before reacting? If we're honest, so much of the unkindness we see and experience isn't rooted in malice—it's rooted in assumptions. We assume someone's tone meant something, or we assume they were trying to offend us. We attach motive to a message, especially in the absence of context.

Text messaging is a perfect example. I use it for simple stuff: "Yes," "No," "Here's a funny meme," or "Check out my Wordle score." But beyond that, it gets murky. A short reply can easily be misread as curt or cold. Without facial expressions or tone, we start to fill in the blanks with our own fears or frustrations, and how unkindness creeps in.

So when it comes to navigating change, one of the first skills we need to build is the ability to reflect. Whether it's a small daily disruption, like the store running out of your favorite flavor of ice cream, or a hurricane that tears through your town, when the moment passes, you need to spend some time in self-reflection. Ask yourself the following:

- How did I respond?
- How did my response make me feel?
- Did I add calm or chaos to the situation?
- Did my response help others, or harm them?
- What could I have done differently?

These questions are powerful at a personal level, but they also apply to businesses and teams trying to do big things in a world of constant disruption.

I have a dear friend who runs a restaurant, and honestly, I can't think of a business more dependent on learning to navigate daily change. She once joked that she could count on two hands the number of days in the last year when *every* staff member scheduled to work actually showed up on time, ready to go. That's real life in the restaurant world.

And the chaos doesn't stop there. Sometimes the meat shipment doesn't arrive. Sometimes a party of six shows up when they only reserved for five, and they're upset that there's no table. Sometimes, a power outage takes out the freezer overnight. It never ends.

The people who succeed—and who lead with kindness through it—are the ones who prepare for the unpredictable. They build systems and procedures that create stability in the middle of the storm. They invest in redundancy, not just for peace of mind, but for sustainability. They cross-train team members so that if someone's out, the job still gets done. In sales and fundraising, we call this "relationship redundancy"—ensuring you've built connections across multiple people and touchpoints so you don't lose a client, donor, or customer when one team member leaves.

Preparation like this matters because navigating change protects relationships and preserves the ability to have an impact. And when change strikes, which it always does, *how* you make decisions becomes as important as *what* you decide.

In her *Harvard Business Review* article "In Uncertain Times, Ask These Questions Before You Make a Decision" (May 2005), Cheryl Strauss Einhorn encourages leaders to approach uncertainty with structured inquiry. She recommends asking targeted questions that help distinguish facts from assumptions, weigh trade-offs, and bring clarity to complex situations. This kind of thinking doesn't make uncertainty go away, but it does create a path forward that's rooted in integrity, not panic. Smart navigation isn't reactive—it's responsive, deliberate, and deeply human.

Her work encourages building processes for navigating chance that are rooted in questions such as:

1. **What do I know for sure?**
   - What's actually happening right now—not what you fear or assume?
   - Is there concrete data?
   - Can I confirm facts with reliable sources?
   - Have I separated facts from assumptions?

2. **What am I assuming?**
   - What are you treating as fact that *may not be?*
   - Are there gaps in information?
   - Is bias or emotion (mine or others) influencing me?
   - What needs to happen to adjust my and/or others' assumptions?

3. **What are my options?**
   - How many pathways, good or bad, can I identify?
   - What is the short-term and long-term impact of each option?
   - Are unexpected or unconventional solutions acceptable?
   - How quickly is action required?

4. **What are the trade-offs? For each option, consider the following:**
   - What am I giving up (i.e., what is the opportunity cost)?
   - Who will be impacted and how?
   - How does the risk balance with reward?

5. **Who else should I involve?**
   - How can I get input from trusted team members or advisers?
   - What are the relationship impacts?
   - Have I invited feedback with humility but boldness?

- Who needs to know that there is a process being used to evaluate options, that there is a decision or plan, and how will that be communicated?

6. **What aligns with your purpose?**
   - Have you checked this decision against your core values?
   - How will you preserve trust and integrity?
   - Will you serve for long-term impact, not short-term control?

Ultimately, you have to figure out what is truly non-negotiable in achieving your goals. What are the core tasks that must be done no matter what? And just as importantly, what are your unbreakable values? These two things—core functions and core values—are your compass.

When change hits, these are the things that will guide you back to center. These are the things that will keep you kind when circumstances get hard, and they're going to be the reason you can look back after a crisis, a delay, or even a disaster and say, "I stayed true to who I am. We stayed true to who we are."

YOU DON'T BUILD MUSCLES BY SITTING STILL

The truth is you don't know how you're going to show up in a moment of disruption until you've lived through it. You can read every leadership book, attend every training, or plan out every possible contingency, but you don't really know how you'll respond to change until you've gone through some deeply personal things.

Real moments of loss, uncertainty, or an unexpected pivot are where your capacity is revealed, but more importantly, that's where it's built. Fear tells us to wait, sit back, and play it safe, but if you never put yourself out there, you'll never develop the muscle to navigate change. You'll never build the resilience that kindness requires.

As we've discussed, one of the greatest challenges of our time is that so much of our modern world is designed to keep us isolated. The algorithms feed us what we already think. Our social feeds show us what we already like, and when we're lonely or discouraged, it's easy to retreat further inward, cocooning ourselves in safety, scrolling through the curated lives of others while slowly disconnecting from our own.

What happens then is that we stop showing up. We stop going on the date or taking the risk. We stop putting ourselves in situations that might stretch us, challenge us, or ask us to be a little braver than we feel. In doing so, we stop growing and developing the tools we'll need when life throws us a curveball.

Kindness in a changing world requires courage, and courage is developed by doing hard things before you feel ready. That means stepping into conversations you're unsure of. It means trying something new even when it scares you, saying yes when fear tells you to say no. Social media wants us to stay in our lane, but that's not where growth lives. It's certainly not where Outrageous Kindness lives.

Outrageous Kindness asks us to stretch, reach across divides, and challenge assumptions. It demands that we stand up and show up for something bigger than ourselves, even if we're not quite sure how it'll go, because the only way to get better at navigating change is to *practice*.

Get in the game. Talk to people who think differently from you. Show up to serve. Try the new thing. Forgive someone. Apologize first. Ask the awkward question. Give generously. Speak kindly, especially when it's hard. That's how you build the muscle, and that's how you make Outrageous Kindness a way of life.

FALLING DOWN TO GET BACK UP

We've had so many conversations with educators lately who are full of worry and heartbreak. What weighs on them most isn't just the curriculum or test scores; it's the pain they feel watching young people struggle to build resilience in a world that rarely asks it of them.

You have to fall down to learn how to get back up, but somewhere along the way, we've forgotten that. We've started cushioning the falls too much. We did it with the best of intentions. Sometimes it takes the form of a parent calling a professor to dispute a grade of D, questioning why their child didn't get the A they were used to. This sort of thing happens more often than you'd think, and as a result, we're sending young adults into the world without the basic muscle of self-reliance. They lack the ability to solve their own problems, let alone help someone else solve theirs.

Resilience isn't built in a vacuum. It's built in the trenches and the discomfort. It comes from the moments when things don't go as planned and no one comes to bail you out. One of the kindest things we can do for others, especially for young people, is let them fail. That's right. Sometimes the most loving, most generous, most growth-inducing gift we can give is a well-earned C or even a D.

We need to normalize failure again. Not everyone is an A student, and frankly, even A students shouldn't expect to get A's all the time. If everything is easy, if everything comes with a gold star, where's the learning? Where's the grit? Where's the stretch?

I'll admit, sometimes I have to bite my tongue when my son comes home venting about a professor who gave critical feedback. There's a part of me that wants to jump in and defend him, to ease the sting, but the wiser part of me—the part that knows growth often comes wrapped in discomfort—reminds me: This is good for him.

Even if the feedback wasn't delivered kindly, even if I disagree with the professor's tone, I'm still grateful for the friction because friction builds strength.

I've told my son more than once, "Bad teachers are a blessing." They show you what *not* to do. They help you recognize the qualities of great teaching. They give you contrast, and contrast brings clarity. One day, when he's in a position to lead or mentor someone else, those hard experiences will shape how he shows up—with more compassion, more patience, and more wisdom.

So, yes, let them get the C or D. Let them have the uncomfortable conversation. Let them sit with the sting of failure or uncertainty. It may not feel kind in the moment, but it's one of the kindest things we can do for our children. We're helping them build the resilience to meet life with both courage and kindness.

YOU HAVE TO EAT THE BROCCOLI

The hardest part of raising a child—or leading a team—is accepting that what you *do* matters more than what you *say*. When it comes to helping others navigate failure, disappointment, or difficult people, your reaction teaches more than your words ever will.

If you want to build resilience in others, you have to live it out in yourself. It's like I tell young parents who ask how to get their kids to eat healthier: If you want them to eat broccoli, you have to eat broccoli.

The same goes for leading teams. If you want your team to handle feedback well, you have to show them how to receive it with humility. If you want them to stay calm under pressure, they need to see you steady in the storm. If you want them to own their mistakes, they have to watch you own yours first. In short, if you want them to eat the broccoli, you have to eat the broccoli. You model the behavior long before you ever ask for it.

THE KINDNESS REQUIRED FOR RESILIENCE

Sometimes the most profound lessons on navigating change aren't found in research, clever frameworks, or business case studies. Sometimes they come in the form of real, raw life.

I remember it vividly. Three months before my fiftieth birthday, I woke up to the news that I had breast cancer. On the day I turned fifty, I began chemotherapy.

What followed was a blur of procedures, including a double mastectomy, chemotherapy, and radiation, but cancer was only the beginning. Six months later, my father passed away. A year after that, my mother grew ill and died. Two months later, my sister suffered a fall and a heart attack, leaving her dependent on hospital care and rehabilitation for nearly a year. And then my husband was diagnosed with Lewy body dementia. Over the next two years, I watched the man I loved fade slowly. All the while, I was raising our son and trying to continue my global philanthropy work.

I don't tell you all of this for sympathy. I tell you because none of it fit into my "worst-case scenario" planning. None of it was predictable, yet I survived it.

Did I always respond with Outrageous Kindness? Honestly, no. There were days when kindness felt like a luxury I couldn't afford, but as I reflect on that relentless decade of change, I can also say this: I found my way through it with a few powerful anchors that helped me keep going and helped me remember who I wanted to be:

STAY CONNECTED TO WHAT YOU VALUE

For me, it was family. Even on the worst days, when fear took over, when pain screamed louder than hope, I knew my family was my *why*. That love grounded me. It gave me something to hold onto when everything else was spinning.

Whatever your values are (love, purpose, faith, contribution), stay connected to them. Let them be your compass when the map disappears.

LET PEOPLE HELP

This one is hard, especially for those of us who are used to being the helper. Navigating change doesn't mean doing it alone. In my case, I had dear friends like Susan who showed up in quiet, unwavering ways. They stood by me, and even though I was terrible at asking for help (I still am), their presence carried me through.

We talk a lot about giving kindness, but receiving it is another muscle entirely. And it's one worth building.

EXTEND GRACE TO OTHERS AND TO YOURSELF

Change is exhausting. You will fumble the ball sometimes. You'll forget to call people back. You'll cry in the grocery store. You'll mess up. Be kind to yourself anyway. Outrageous Kindness means choosing to return over and over again to grace, growth, and love.

REMEMBER WHAT MAKES NAVIGATING HARD AND CHOOSE TO PRACTICE ANYWAY

Change is hard because it strips us of predictability. It threatens our sense of safety and awakens the fear of failure. Let's face it: We care about what others think when we take a wrong turn, often too much.

An often-paraphrased quote from Theodore Roosevelt's "Man in the Arena" speech: "Unless you're in the ring with me, getting bloody, I don't care what you think." That's easier said than done because we're social creatures who define ourselves through others, but it's still a truth worth holding onto.

Ultimately, navigating change is about realigning with your values. It's about becoming the kind of person who can respond with purpose even in the middle of a struggle. We don't build that muscle by thinking about it. We build it by living through it. And when we do—when we get through just one day, one hour, one breath at a time—we discover that Outrageous Kindness isn't something we reach for *after* the storm. It's the light we carry *through* it.

THE STRENGTH IN ASKING AND THE POWER IN FINISHING

One of the hardest sentences I've ever had to say out loud is, "I need help." It's not because I didn't have people who loved me or that I lacked support. I was simply too proud, and I thought resilience meant doing everything alone.

It doesn't. If you truly want to learn how to navigate change, you have to be humble enough to admit, "I can't do this by myself." That's where kindness begins—not just the kindness you offer to others, but the kindness you allow for yourself. The kindness that says, "You're still strong, even when you ask for help." The kindness that believes community is part of the design and not a crutch.

As you walk through seasons of transition, whether grief, illness, uncertainty, or stress, connection becomes your oxygen. Stay rooted in your purpose, build a circle of support, and allow others to walk beside you. That's not weakness. It's wisdom.

There's something else I've found to be powerfully healing during the most painful and unpredictable changes of my life: achieving a goal, no matter how small, in spite of everything.

During my cancer treatment, there were days I could barely lift my head, but if, after four hours of chemo, I managed to send a memo my client needed or help move their project forward, it made a big difference. That one small accomplishment reminded me that I still had something to give and my identity wasn't reduced to the pain I was in.

Some of my most joyful moments, believe it or not, were when I wore a wig to meetings with people who had no idea I was undergoing chemotherapy. I'd show up fully present, talking strategy, thinking creatively, giving advice. I wasn't trying to hide my suffering—I wanted to transcend it. Not to deny the pain, but to defy its power over me.

One of my favorite stories in the Bible tells of a paralyzed man who was carried by his friends to a house so packed with people that they couldn't get through the door. They wanted to bring him to Jesus so he might be healed—that was the goal, but accomplishing it seemed almost impossible. So they dug a hole in the roof and lowered him down. When Jesus saw the faith of this man and his friends, he didn't offer a dramatic speech. He simply said, "Pick up your mat and walk."[17]

In other words, don't stay stuck. Don't wait for perfect. Stand up and do the next thing you can do.

That story lives in me, especially in those years when everything seemed to fall apart. The ability to do *just one thing,* to complete a small task, restored my sense of agency. It reminded me that while I couldn't control the storm, I could still move through it with intention.

When everything feels out of control, focus on finishing *something.* Send the email. Fold the laundry. Write the note. Pick up the phone. It might seem small, but it's proof that you are still here and still moving forward. Often, that small act will become the very thing that lifts you up, dusts you off, and gives you the courage to keep walking. And that is the heart of Navigate.

CHAPTER 6

D—Deliver

BY THE TIME we reach the final letter in the KIND Method—*D for Deliver*—we've already committed to *Know more*, we've defined the *Impact* we want to make, and we've learned how to *Navigate* the unexpected twists and turns of life. But without *Delivery*, without follow-through, all of that is just theory. It's not real until we act on it.

Delivering means we take what we know, what we feel, and what we hope for, and we do something about it. Real change, whether personal, professional, or relational, isn't the result of one sweeping, cinematic gesture. It's built from small, deliberate acts, day after day. You don't wake up one morning and decide to get in shape, and by the next morning, magically arrive there. Transformation takes work. The same is true of kindness, especially Outrageous Kindness. It takes consistent, intentional effort.

In a world where we're constantly flooded with "thoughts and prayers," doing something is radical. I'm not against expressing compassionate thoughts, and I'm certainly not against prayer. However, kindness must move from sentiment to substance, and that is what Deliver is all about.

Now, to be clear, delivery doesn't always mean delivering *success.* The KIND Method was never about perfection—it's about showing up even when the work is hard, and even when you fall short. Sometimes, that means doing what you said you'd do and taking responsibility for the outcome, not shifting blame or leaving others to pick up the slack.

One of the kindest things we can do in any community is to follow through. If you agree to lead a project, show up for the meetings. If you volunteer to help, follow through with effort and energy. Nothing erodes trust faster than failing to deliver, and few things are more quietly cruel than letting others carry the burden of our forgotten or abandoned commitments.

In fact, delivery builds trust, and trust is the currency of every meaningful relationship. Whether it's a customer, a marriage, a team, a philanthropic donor, or a friendship, without trust, nothing sticks and nothing lasts.

There are decades of research to back this up. The longest-running happiness study, Harvard's famous longitudinal project that began in 1938, continues to reaffirm this truth: *Meaningful relationships are the strongest predictor of lifelong happiness.*[18] Strong relationships don't happen by accident. They're built through consistency, reliability, and the kind of delivery that says, "You can count on me."

As Susan puts it, "We are always writing the story of our lives, and many of us are stuck in old scripts and stories we've been telling ourselves for years." The same loop keeps running through our heads: *I'm not disciplined enough. I can't finish what I start. I don't have what it takes. People like me don't do things like that.*

If you're stuck on that script, delivering on even one small goal will help you rewrite the story. With every follow-through, you create a new chapter. With every small victory, you will begin to believe in your own capacity to finish what you start.

However, it's about more than personal growth. Delivering is also about earning the opportunity for greater impact. In business, entrepreneurs who deliver for their customers and investors gain more capital and trust. In philanthropy, nonprofits that report results and keep their promises attract more donors and build broader community support.

Delivering means also being honest about what's possible. Set deadlines and honor them. Ask for help when needed. Focus on what's *essential* rather than what's just "nice to have." That's the daily discipline of commitment. Above all, delivering reinforces our humanity by grounding us in the truth that kindness isn't just how we *feel* but what we *do*.

So take the step. Finish the project. Write the thank-you note. Offer the solution. Keep your word. Kindness only transforms the world when we Deliver.

WHY DELIVERING IS SO HARD

Delivering on a promise, a goal, or even a small task sounds simple, and yet in real life, it's often the hardest part. Life rarely unfolds in a neat, orderly fashion. Remember my friend who owns a restaurant? She could give you a mile-long list of reasons why plans fall apart: Deliveries don't arrive; staff members call in sick; power goes out; customers show up late, early, or with unexpected requests. You name it; it happens.

And that's exactly why *Navigate* comes before *Deliver.* In order to follow through, we have to accept that life *won't* go according to plan. We have to build the muscle of adaptation. Life throws curveballs daily, and delivering despite them is part of the practice of Outrageous Kindness.

Beyond the chaos of daily life, there's a deeper reason people struggle to deliver: *lack of clarity.* In organizations, businesses, and even our personal lives, one of the most common (and avoidable) barriers to delivering is not being totally sure what we're trying to deliver in the first place. And that's why the *I* in KIND—*Impact*—is so important. If we're unclear about the outcome we're working toward, how will we ever know if we've succeeded?

I see this often in the fundraising world. People in development roles frequently say, "I'm here to build relationships." While that's absolutely true, it's not the whole story. The development function of a nonprofit exists to secure resources, but without clear expectations around results, that purpose can quickly become muddled. If relationships aren't helping to raise essential funds, engage donors more deeply, or open doors to transformational support, the organization will face significant challenges. Ultimately, if those relationships don't move the mission forward, then the development team isn't delivering on what matters most.

This doesn't just happen in nonprofits. In corporate settings, high achievers are often asked to take on extra assignments. At first, they're flattered. Then they're overloaded. Eventually, they feel frustrated and burned out. They've become so busy doing *everything* that they're no longer clear on what they were hired to deliver in the first place.

One of the kindest things we can do, for ourselves and others, is to seek clarity. To ask, *What are we really trying to accomplish? What is the essential outcome here?* And if that clarity isn't handed to us, we must be willing to go ask for it—over and over again, if necessary, because when we don't clarify, we drift. We rationalize and blame. We say things like, "Well, my boss wasn't clear," or "I thought they wanted me to focus on this instead." And suddenly, we're off course. We're working hard, but we aren't working in the right direction.

Delivering means doing the right things, not just staying busy. It means cutting through distractions, checking our assumptions, and getting real about what matters most.

THE HEARTBEAT OF OUTRAGEOUS KINDNESS

When I was growing up, I had a front-row seat to the world of inspiration. Because of the work my father did, I was regularly surrounded by what I now think of as world-class motivational speakers, some of whom had their own television shows and audiences who hung on every word. Their messages were often filled with passion, vision, and belief. They could light up a room with hope, and for a long time, I thought that's all it took. If you believed hard enough and spoke positively enough, life would change.

What I know now is that, while belief is essential and intent matters, without action—without *Delivering*—our best intentions never take root. They're never validated, tested, or strengthened. They remain ideas floating in our heads and hearts, disconnected from the world that needs them most.

You can Know more (K), define your Impact (I), and learn to Navigate the inevitable ups and downs (N), but if you never *do* anything, you'll never bridge the gap between how you're living and how you *want* to live. That gap is a place of frustration that gnaws at your peace of mind because you *know* you're meant for something more. You *know* you're meant to live kindly, boldly, outrageously, but you haven't delivered.

Delivering is the part of kindness that says, "Yes, this matters enough to act on." You might fail seventeen times along the way, but showing up and trying again is what creates the change you're craving. So when people say, "I want to live a kinder life," my question is always, "What are you actually doing to make that happen?"

Again, it's easy to send thoughts and prayers. Those things are good and meaningful, but ultimately, Outrageous Kindness lives in *how you act*. It's how you show up in a crisis, how you follow through on promises, how you treat people when no one's watching. It's how you listen. How you lead. How you love.

I've been around a lot of incredibly visionary people with big dreams and powerful messages, and some were better at *talking* about change than actually *creating* it. Talk is easy. Follow-through is what transforms lives.

That's why I often say, "Stop talking. Start doing." In fact, that's how one of my businesses was born. My late husband and I kept talking about how we wanted to make fundraising and philanthropy best practices more accessible to smaller, grassroots nonprofits. We had a thousand conversations about it, and finally, driving home from a trip, I turned to him and said, "We either need to do something about this or stop talking about it."

That moment of decision, that line in the sand, is the essence of *Deliver*. It's what moves ideas from theory into impact.

Even in everyday life, this principle shows up. If the same traffic jam makes you miserable every morning, what's the kindest thing you can do for yourself *and* for others on the road? Keep complaining and become an aggressive driver who spreads that frustration around? Or find a new route? Maybe leave earlier? Sometimes, the right action is incredibly simple.

So the *D* in KIND reminds us to dream boldly and believe deeply, but above all, *deliver*. It doesn't have to be perfect, or always on time, but do it consistently and with love. That's how kindness becomes real in the world.

NEAR-TERM IMPACT

It's easier to get started on delivering when you have an *imminent* timeframe in mind. We often set starting points that are too far into the future, which makes change easier to think about but also easier to procrastinate. For example, it's a lot easier to think in terms of what we want to change a year from now. A year feels comfortably distant. It gives us plenty of time to dream without demanding action. We don't have to take that first step because we have all the time in the world.

Unfortunately, in this day and age, where media attention shifts in the blink of an eye, you don't have to wait long before the pressure to act evaporates altogether as something else captures everyone's attention. For that reason, I usually ask the teams I work with, "What do you want to have changed thirty days from now, and what will be different in sixty or ninety days?" Setting milestones at thirty, sixty, or even ninety days makes action imminent, rather than pushing it off to some faraway date.

Early in my career, I worked with someone who was endlessly generous with advice and support. He was wise, thoughtful, full of clever phrases and affirmations. We often went out to lunch together, and every time, without fail, he would order an enormous amount of food, enthusiastically enjoying every bite. Just before dessert arrived, he would look at me with a smile and say, "I start my diet Monday."

He never said *which* Monday. It was always just *some* Monday.

It still makes me laugh to this day, because we all do this in some way. We all have our own version of "I'll start my diet

Monday." Maybe it's, "I'll be more generous once I get that raise." Or, "I'll start volunteering when work calms down." Or, "I'll begin saving once I pay off this debt."

The truth is that "Monday" often never comes. Unless we commit to action today, we risk letting our best intentions slip into the ether of "someday." That's why defining *near-term impact* is so important. What do you want to have accomplished in the next thirty days? Sixty days? Ninety days? What small shift will move you closer to the life and kindness you envision within that relatively short timeframe?

Living with kindness means living with intention. It means asking not just what you care about, but what you're doing about it. Are you starting the diet today? Are you showing up, even in small ways, for the things and people you value today? Let's not wait until some mysterious Monday.

When I was building my first startup, I often felt overwhelmed by the sheer number of things to do. That's when I created what I now call the "Three Things" approach to my day. In the next section, I'll explain why making a connection to your purpose should always be the first item on your list. After that, I would identify the two most important tasks I needed to accomplish and set a goal to complete them by noon. I didn't always hit that mark, but I always made meaningful progress. And that consistent focus moved both me and the company closer to hitting our sales goals, meeting product development deadlines, and executing our broader strategy.

DELIVERING BEFORE NOON EVERY DAY

Delivering on kindness doesn't require a grand gesture. You don't need to launch a nonprofit or reinvent your career overnight.

The real magic of delivery lies in what you do with your everyday moments.

Start each day by reconnecting with your *I*—your Impact. Of course, some mornings are harder than others. You might be struggling with uncertainty, grief, frustration, or burnout today. When that happens, your kindness practice becomes even more important. If you can't easily connect to your purpose in those moments, try reaching out to someone who reminds you who you are. Ask for support, and if that feels too vulnerable, do something simple and kind for a stranger. There's healing in generosity. Sometimes, the best way to reconnect with our own impact is to extend it to someone else.

You can also build a simple ritual. Each morning, ask yourself why you're doing what you do. What do you love about your work? What brings you joy in the role you play in your family or community? Then act on it. Do one thing before noon that connects you to that deeper purpose.

Here's where we borrow a bit of wisdom from Mark Twain. He once said, "If it's your job to eat a frog, it's best to do it first thing in the morning. That way, it's the worst thing you'll face all day."[19]

I would like to flip that idea. If you want to live with more Outrageous Kindness, start your day with your best act. Begin with something meaningful, even if it's small. Write a thank-you note. Compliment someone. Let the other driver go first at the stop sign—yes, even when traffic is maddening. Stop and listen to that annoying coworker or smile at someone who always feels grumpy.

Whatever task or conversation you've been putting off, do it first. Let kindness lead your calendar. When you prioritize kindness early in the day, everything else tends to flow more freely, and that makes delivering on kindness a habit.

So tomorrow morning, ask yourself, *What one thing can I do before noon that will keep me connected to my purpose?* Then go do it. That's how Outrageous Kindness begins.

WHAT YOU GAIN WHEN YOU DELIVER

So, what do you actually gain from practicing Deliver? A lot.

First and foremost, you begin writing a new story about yourself. When you actually deliver on the things you've said you were going to do, you start proving something powerful to yourself: *Yes, I can change. Yes, I can grow. Yes, I can create the life I want.* It begins with keeping promises, first to yourself and then to others. Those small, quiet acts of follow-through start building momentum until you realize you are capable of real, purpose-driven success.

The second benefit is *social capital,* which we discussed earlier. We all understand financial capital. It's the difference between what you own and what you owe. It's your net worth on paper. Social capital, on the other hand, is the web of relationships and trust that surrounds you. It's the support system that holds you up when life knocks you down. Remember, as that long-running study from Harvard University showed, social capital is one of the single greatest predictors of a joyful, fulfilling life.

And guess how you gain even more social capital? You deliver. You show up when you say you will, keep your word, and do the kind thing. When people know they can count on you, their trust in you deepens, and the relationship grows stronger. That creates a ripple effect in your own life, your workplace, your home, your community, and beyond.

Happiness and high performance don't come from pressure or fear. They come from joy, kindness, and connection. The more you deliver Outrageous Kindness as a way of life, the more peace, confidence, and happiness you'll find.

In other words, *Deliver* isn't just about getting things done. It's about building the life, relationships, and legacy that matter most. It's how we bring the KIND Method to life and help shape a world that works better for everyone.

Activating Kindness by Delivering

These actions bring the KIND Method full circle and demonstrate how delivery activates kindness as a lived practice:

- **Be a Hobbit:** Take consistent, small actions to turn knowledge and intention into impact. Follow-through is what makes kindness real.
- **Get a Job:** Start where you are. Follow through on commitments, no matter how small, in your community, work, and relationships to build trust, which is the foundation of happiness and social capital.
- **Clarify What You're Delivering:** Vagueness leads to misalignment and burnout. Ask what truly matters.
- **Avoid Starting on "Monday":** Set near-term goals (thirty, sixty, ninety days) to avoid deferring action to "someday" or "Monday."

- **Eat the Frog:** Start each day with a focus on your purpose and small steps that will get you to your outrageous goals. Let it lead your calendar and create daily momentum.
- **Check a Box for Yourself:** Keep promises to yourself first to build belief, confidence, and a new story about who you are becoming.
- **Eat the Broccoli:** Prioritize action over talk. Outrageous Kindness lives in what you do, not what you say.
- **Ask Strategic Questions:** Deliver even when life is messy. Navigate disruptions, ask for help, and adapt with purpose.
- **Strengthen Social Capital:** Use delivery to strengthen social capital. People trust those who follow through.

CHAPTER 7

D—Dance

IT'S TIME TO let you in on a little secret.

The letter *D* in the KIND Method actually stands for two things. That's right. It stands for *Deliver*, but it also stands for *Dance*. When we first created the KIND Method, we had some lively debates about whether we should even include the second D. As we started working on this book, we considered tucking it away quietly in another chapter, like an unspoken ingredient in a recipe.

In the end, we made a bold choice to give Dance its own chapter and treat it as an integral part of the whole. After all, Dance isn't just something extra. It's the energy that underlies the entire KIND Method. It's not a step you do after the real work is done—it's the spirit that carries you through every step of the journey.

One of the kindest things you can do, especially in moments of stress or difficulty, is to bring joy into a room. When the atmosphere is heavy, when people are angry, overwhelmed, or afraid, someone who brings a smile, a laugh, or a moment of levity is doing sacred work. Laughter disarms fear, and joy disrupts despair. A sense of humor, especially in leadership, is a superpower, and it's deeply kind.

Dance, in this context, is not necessarily about music or movement (though it certainly can be). It's about *lightness*. It's about not taking yourself too seriously. It's about showing up in a way that reminds people, even in hard times, that life is still worth celebrating. There is beauty, connection, and playfulness to be found even when things are far from perfect.

Think about the *K* in KIND—*Know more*. Well, part of knowing more is knowing people, and that means really seeing them, taking time to listen, laugh, and engage with them. Dance is what makes knowing others a joyful experience, not just an intellectual exercise.

Or consider the *I—Impact*. Dance reminds us that the impact we make is amplified when people actually *enjoy* working with us. In business, in philanthropy, in teams of all kinds, leaders who bring joy tend to attract better talent, build stronger cultures, and create lasting results. Research in sports psychology backs this up. Athletes who *enjoy* what they do consistently outperform those who don't.[20]

Take Olympic ski racer Lindsey Vonn. She is the only American woman to win an Olympic downhill gold and the only one to claim four World Cup overall titles. Her accomplishments are staggering, but behind every medal were countless falls, failures, and fears. And yet, she's known not just for her dominance on the slopes but for her mindset off of them.

"If you go around being afraid," she said, "you're never going to enjoy life. You have only one chance, so you've got to have fun."

Lindsey decided that, instead of focusing on the pressure, she would focus on having fun. That mindset shift changed everything. Her performance soared once she embraced the joy of skiing.

Strategies built on fear can never sustain success. Stress may propel you for a moment, but it will eventually deplete you. On the other hand, joy endures. It fuels us in a way fear never can.

Recent research from consulting firm Kearney highlights how joy in the workplace—yes, even in corporate environments—improves performance, harmony, and results.[21] I'll never forget visiting a Chicago nonprofit called the Cara Initiative. They help people facing serious life challenges to deal with unexplainable gaps in their résumés and get into their first real jobs. Every single morning, the entire office gathered to share something they'd learned or something that brought them joy. It was a simple but profound exercise. That daily act of choosing joy, of finding something worth smiling about, became a cornerstone of their culture.

That same week, I happened to watch a post-Super Bowl interview. The reporters asked one of the star players how this championship compared to his last. He paused and said something I'll never forget: "The first time I played in the Super Bowl, I was so focused on performing well, on winning, that I didn't enjoy it. I was tense. I didn't play my best. This time, I made the decision that I was going to have fun. I'd still play hard. I'd still give it my all. But I was going to enjoy the moment that I had spent my whole life dreaming about and working for."

That's the Dance. It's remembering to celebrate the journey and make space for levity, even as we push toward our goals. After all, if we're working hard to create a kinder, more purposeful life but never stopping to enjoy it, what's the point?

So, yes, we included a second *D* in KIND (or, perhaps, KINDD?). Not because it's extra, but because it's *vitally important.* Joy isn't a luxury—it's fuel, and kindness without joy is just obligation in disguise. Kindness should feel good, and life, even at its hardest, deserves to be lived with heart, humor, and a little music in your soul.

DANCE UNLOCKS FLOW

Enjoyment, laughter, movement, music—these aren't distractions from the serious work of life. They are enhancers of it. They help us achieve more than we ever imagined because they help unlock a mental state psychologists call *flow*—that almost magical condition where effort feels effortless, and we're completely immersed in the task at hand. I was just talking with my son about this the other day. He's a musician, and one of his friends, an absolutely brilliant percussionist, had just experienced one of the worst performances of his life. It was a juried performance for a grade, so the stakes were high, and the pressure was intense. In the middle of it, this otherwise flawless performer skipped over thirty full measures of the song. He just blew past them without even realizing.

How does that happen? How can someone so skilled, so prepared, fall apart in the moment? My son and I unpacked it together, and like so many of life's challenges, it came down to frame of mind. Joy had left. Stress and fear had taken its place, and they hijacked his ability to be present, to flow. This is a little of the Self One (the teller) and Self Two (the doer) from Gallwey as well.

This is the quiet, radical power of Dance. I always tell my son, when you're performing, whether it's on a stage or in a meeting, you're not just communicating facts or talent. You are sharing emotion. So I asked him, "What do you want me to feel when I hear you play? Do you want me to feel your anxiety? Or do you want me to feel the joy of the music you love?"

That same question applies to leaders. What do you want the people around you to feel? Do you want your team to absorb your stress and fear? Or do you want them to feel your energy, your commitment, your belief, your joy?

Great leaders carry joy with them—not fake cheer or forced positivity, but deep, resilient joy that creates connection and momentum even in hard times. That's what the *D* of Dance is really about.

Just to be clear, I'm not talking about superficial attempts at "team-building." I think we all have stories about company events where everyone is supposed to bond over cupcakes and personality tests. There's that famous episode of *The Office* where the team spends an absurd amount of time trying to decide what kind of cake to buy for a birthday party, and in the end, no one really feels seen or celebrated. That's not the kind of dance we mean.

Real Dance is about authentic joy. It's about passion for the work. It's about the spark you bring into a room, the resilience to laugh through the mess, the ability to keep moving because you remember that life is still good, even in the struggle.

Celebration only works when it's *real.* Authenticity is what gives joy its power. Whether as individuals or organizations, we can't fake kindness, and we can't fake joy. True joy comes from aligning our actions with our values. It comes from knowing that the good we do is rooted in something meaningful, not performative.

In a nonprofit or organizational setting, this matters tremendously. We often feel the pressure to "do the expected"—to send the birthday card, host the event, send the thank-you email. While often these things have value, they don't move people the way real, lived impact does. The most powerful way to honor someone's generosity is not with a plaque but with a story. Show them the life that was changed because of their gift. Let them *see* the ripple effect of their kindness. That's what ignites joy.

In their research *Joy at Work*, A. T. Kearney breaks joy down into three key elements: *harmony*, *impact*, and *acknowledgment*. These are not just workplace principles—they're human ones. Harmony means creating environments where people know how to feel safe and want to bring all of their talent and perspectives to the work. Impact is knowing the work you're doing matters. And acknowledgment is being seen, heard, and appreciated for that work.

So, as you reflect on how to live with more joy and how to lead with more kindness, remember this: Celebration isn't the *extra*. It's the *essential*. It's how we honor what we value, how we nourish what we've built, and how we write a story that others will want to be part of.

JOY MUST BE FELT

In a recent reflection on joy in Black philanthropy, Rochelle Jerry noted that the act of giving, when it flows from deep cultural and personal truth, becomes its own form of celebration. It's a way of saying, "This matters. I matter. My story matters."[22] This insight doesn't just apply to donors or nonprofits—it applies to all of us. When we give from a place of joy, we create a cycle of purpose and renewal that carries us forward.

For organizations, this means you can't choreograph someone else's joy. You can make space for it. You can support it. You can reflect it back through stories and transparency, but ultimately, each person must find their own reason to dance.

The best thing you can do is to stop trying to control the performance and start trusting in the music. Let your team members, your supporters, your partners discover what brings *them* joy and connects *them* to purpose. Joy cannot be forced. It must be *felt*.

So choose to dance even on the hard days. *Especially* on the hard days.

When I was undergoing treatment for breast cancer, I realized just how vital joy was. I learned that joy was not something you waited for on the other side of healing. It was something you had to bring with you *through* the healing.

At the time of this writing, I am approaching my ten-year checkup. Ten years. I'll finally be finished with all medications, which is a huge milestone. As I look back, I can say with certainty that Dance mattered. Laughter, even in the chemo room, mattered. These things kept me connected to life and constantly reminded me who I was, even when everything around me was uncertain.

That's what Dance does. It grounds us and lifts us at the same time. For that reason, it is one of the kindest gifts we can give to others and to ourselves. So, whether you lead a team, raise a family, serve in a community, or simply show up for your own dreams, don't forget the Dance. Let joy move through you. Let it steady your hands, soften your voice, and remind you that purpose and play are not opposites. They belong together.

DANCE PARTIES IN THE MIDDLE OF THE STORM

My son was in third grade when I was getting chemotherapy and radiation. At the time, I was also running two businesses. In other words, I had a few things going on. Between doctor visits, treatments, and trying to keep my companies afloat, life felt like a tsunami I was trying to out-swim.

Thankfully, my middle sister came to stay with us during that time. She stepped in with the kind of quiet strength and deep love that only a sister can offer. She helped take care of my son, managed the house, and just kept things running while I focused on getting through.

One night, I called home to check in, and I could hear loud music blasting in the background. It was chaos. "What on earth is going on?" I asked her. "He's in third grade! Has he done his homework? Is he getting ready for bed? Why is there music playing at this hour?"

And she just laughed. "It's a dance party," she said.

"Dance party?" I asked, trying to wrap my mind around it.

"Yeah. We have a dance party every night."

I paused, probably still wearing my "serious mom" voice. "What do you mean *every* night?"

She explained. "Look. All day long, people keep asking him how you are. 'Is your mom OK? How's she doing? Is she going to be all right?' He hears it over and over again at school, at home, at church. He can't escape it, so I figured, at least for part of the night, we need to do something that's not about cancer. Something fun. Something loud and silly. So every night before bed, we crank up the music, run around the house, and dance."

She probably let him jump on the furniture, too, though I didn't ask. And honestly, I didn't need to, because the truth is, she was right. That nightly dance party wasn't just a distraction. It was a healing ritual. A defiant act of joy in the middle of fear. It was how my son learned to cope with something too big for his young heart to hold. It was how our family found breath when the air had been knocked out of us.

Dance is about reclaiming joy in the middle of pain. It's what helps us navigate (there's that *N* again) when life throws its worst at us. It's how we remember that laughter still belongs to us, even when the world feels dark. Dance reminds us that joy doesn't have to wait for everything to be perfect. Joy *is* the strength that helps us keep going when everything's not.

My sister didn't just give my son a fun moment. She gave him a tool and taught him that in the hardest seasons, you're still allowed to celebrate life. That joy is not just for the easy days. It's for the days when you need it most.

Yes, we've talked a lot about dance in a metaphorical sense as a joyful mindset, an ability to bring levity into tough moments, and the power of helping others smile through difficulty. But let's not overlook the *literal* value of dancing, either.

According to A. T. Kearney, taking a simple dance break during the day can completely reset your mindset. Movement, music, and a few minutes of just letting go can improve your attitude, boost your productivity, and bring your spirit back online. My sister instinctively knew this when she started those nightly dance parties with my son. She didn't have a study or a methodology—she just knew he needed joy. He needed a break from the heaviness, so she turned up the music and made space for joy. That's *Dance* in action.

I've carried that lesson with me ever since. I can't tell you how many times I've raced off a terrible flight, dragging my carry-on through some overcrowded airport, only to pop in my earbuds, crank up the music, and jam my way to the next gate. It changes everything. The rhythm cuts through the stress. The music drowns out the frustration. Suddenly, I'm smiling again, and I'm back to who I want to be.

Even if it's just a quick shuffle in a grocery store aisle because they play the best music (my favorite part of grocery shopping) or a secret dance party in the bathroom stall (you'd be surprised how often that happens)—whatever it looks like, give yourself permission to reset.

You don't have to be good at it. You just need to move. Wherever you are in your journey, don't forget the dance party. Don't forget that joy can be both protest and prayer. Turn it up. Let it out. Dance like your healing depends on it.

THE JOY OF SHOWING UP

Progress rarely happens all at once. Purpose-driven success isn't a single moment of glory. It's a million small steps, and if we don't stop to celebrate those steps along the way, the road can start to feel impossibly long.

That's why celebration is a core part of both *Deliver* and *Dance* in the KIND Method. Not only should we begin each morning by reconnecting to our purpose and the impact we want to make, but we also need to end each day with a moment of reflection and gratitude. Celebration is how we stay motivated when the vision is huge and the distance to the goal feels overwhelming.

I'll give you an example. One of our goals is to spread Outrageous Kindness to one million people. That's a big number. It's the kind of thing that could easily feel daunting if we only looked at how far we still have to go, but instead, we celebrate *every single one*. Every person who joins the movement, every message we receive, every story someone shares is one more step toward a million that's worth celebrating.

If we wait to cheer until the mountain is fully climbed, we'll miss the beauty of the journey, but if we pause to recognize each foothold, each tiny win, we'll find the energy to keep going. Celebration sustains us.

Right now, we're encouraging people in our community not just to do acts of kindness but to notice and lift up the kindness they see around them. We're asking them to capture those moments of random, real, beautiful things they see others doing and share them. The purpose is to amplify joy by reminding us all that kindness is alive and often hiding in plain sight. We just need to pay attention.

One word of caution here: Nobody wants fake fun. We've all been in those environments where the "fun" feels forced and everyone's just going through the motions. That's not the kind of celebration we're talking about. Real joy is authentic. Real celebration is rooted in genuine connection and purpose. It's not about balloons and confetti (though those can be fun too). It's about acknowledging what matters.

Don't wait for the big finish. Celebrate your kindness in action. Celebrate your growth. Celebrate someone else's goodness. Most of all, celebrate the fact that you're showing up with joy, heart, and courage to make a difference.

So, yes, Dance is part of the KIND Method for a reason. It's the joy that sustains the mission. It's the spark that fuels our energy. It's the reminder that no matter how serious life gets, we are still allowed to *celebrate*.

Dance, dance, dance—not because it fixes everything, but because it helps you remember what you're fighting for.

CHAPTER 8

Tools for Practicing Outrageous Kindness

OUTRAGEOUS KINDNESS ISN'T a viral moment or a line in your obituary. It's a choice you make day after day until it becomes the rhythm of your life. So, how do you practice it, especially in a world that often rewards speed, efficiency, and cynicism more than compassion?

You start small. You stay consistent. And you let kindness become your default, not your exception.

Here are a few daily, weekly, and long-term practices that can help you cultivate a life of Outrageous Kindness:

Ask for Something Every Day

Yes, *ask*. Kindness begins with connection, and connection begins with vulnerability. When you ask for help, input, a fresh perspective, or simply someone else's voice at the table, you're building relationships rooted in trust. You're signaling that you don't have to do it all alone, and neither does anyone else.

Asking creates space and builds social capital. It keeps burnout at bay. It reminds you that generosity is a two-way street, so make it a daily habit to ask. In doing so, you are building interdependence.

Thank Someone Every Day—Meaningfully

In a world full of automatic "thanks" and thumbs-up emojis, heartfelt gratitude can feel rare. That's why it matters so much.

Get into the habit of noticing and naming the good others bring into your life. Say thank you for the things that cost people something, whether it's their time, their thoughtfulness, their courage, or something else. Don't just keep it to yourself. Speak it out loud. Send the note. Share the moment.

During my cancer treatment, I quickly learned that gratitude was medicine, and part of my emotional healing depended on staying connected to what I was most thankful for. That practice of giving thanks out loud changed me. Studies have shown that mindful gratitude journaling in cancer patients significantly reduces psychological distress and suffering while improving quality of life, and that ongoing gratitude practice fosters resilience, strengthens relationships, and supports post-traumatic growth during even the hardest seasons.[23]

Highlight the Good in Others

We live in a world where the bad news always breaks faster than the good, but Outrageous Kindness flips that script.

One way we're doing this is through the *Outrageous Kindness Meter*—a platform where people can spotlight the good they see in others. We want to amplify stories that might otherwise go unnoticed: the stranger who helped, the leader who listened, the child who shared.

You can do this in your everyday life as well. See a post about someone doing something good? Re-share it. Witness a moment of compassion? Tell someone about it. Let your social media feed reflect the kind of world you want to help build, not just the one that's screaming loudest.

Invite Someone in

One of the greatest acts of kindness is extending an invitation, so ask someone to walk with you, share a meal, attend an event, sit beside you, or join your joy. You don't need a reason beyond togetherness.

Recently, I saw a great example of this. My beautiful friend and accomplished poet, Beth Ann Fennelly, hosted a quiet reading circle in a local coffee shop. There was no agenda, no discussion prompts, just people bringing their own books and reading silently together. The result was community and connection.

In a world that feels increasingly fragmented, we need more of that. Outrageous Kindness often looks like choosing inclusion, especially for those who don't usually get the invite.

Use Your Voice to Forward the Good

Finally, think about how you use your platform, whatever that looks like. Whether you have ten followers or ten thousand, your voice can make a difference. Instead of joining the outrage machine or doom-scrolling in despair, become a beacon. Share what's working. Praise what's noble. Point to what's possible.

The internet doesn't need more cynics. It needs more storytellers of kindness. Our phones buzz constantly with breaking news, heated arguments, and endless opinions, but what if we used that same digital reach to build something beautiful? What if kindness, not outrage, became the most contagious thing on the internet?

That's exactly the vision behind the Outrageous Kindness movement. We believe that Outrageous Kindness isn't just a feel-good idea. It's a mindset, a method, and a movement, and like all movements, it thrives on connection. That's why one of the simplest yet most powerful things you can do is to become part of the community online. Follow Outrageous Kindness on Instagram. Read the stories, share your own, and repost the moments that inspire you. Our dream is to gather one million people who are practicing Outrageous Kindness together, and it starts with you.

But it doesn't stop there. Part of living out Outrageous Kindness is supporting the people and causes that move your heart. If clean water matters to you, find and follow organizations that are working on that front. If your soul stirs for animal welfare, or you ache for at-risk children, or you're passionate about education, justice, or public health—support the nonprofits, initiatives, and advocates working in those areas.

Don't underestimate the impact of something as simple as a repost or a thoughtful comment. Nonprofits and purpose-driven groups need more than just donations—they need visibility. They need people who will amplify their voice and help shape a more informed, compassionate public. The root causes of injustice often go beyond a lack of money. They're rooted in belief systems, social behaviors, and generational mindsets that must change, and your voice—your social feed—can help change them.

So if you care deeply about something, show it. Share the stories. Elevate the voices. Use your digital platform, no matter how big or small, to lift up the good. Being part of the Outrageous Kindness movement means choosing to flood your digital world with grace, compassion, and possibility. You don't have to change the whole world today, but you can help light it up one post, one story, one act at a time.

These practices aren't complex. They don't require perfection or a massive time commitment. What they require is a willingness to see, honor, invite, and act. That's the heart of Outrageous Kindness: not dramatic gestures, but repeated choices that say, "You matter. We belong. This can be better."

Start where you are. Choose one practice, repeat it, and watch what grows.

Track Your Kindness Journey

Most of us don't need one more complicated checklist to add to our already full lives. The point of Outrageous Kindness is not perfection. It's movement and awareness. It's choosing to show up, again and again, in a world that desperately needs more love and less noise.

So, how do we actually *track* a kindness journey, especially one that asks us to lean into bold, often uncomfortable acts of compassion? We keep it simple. I've found that three small but intentional practices can make a huge difference.

1. **Set clear, personal goals**—Outrageous Kindness doesn't happen by accident. It begins with intention. Ask yourself: Where do I want to make a change? Maybe it's reaching out to three people a week just to lift their spirits. Maybe it's being kinder to yourself in moments of failure. Maybe it's choosing to speak up when you normally stay silent, or staying curious when you'd rather judge. Whatever it is, make it real, make it yours, and write it down.

2. **Check in with yourself monthly**—Once a month—maybe when you sit down to do your finances or plan your schedule—pause and reflect. Ask yourself, *How did I do? Where did I stretch? Where did I fall short?* Celebrate what went well, and adjust what didn't. Be gentle with yourself. This isn't about keeping score. It's about staying awake to your own growth. What we measure, we tend to improve.

3. **Look for kindness in others**—Tracking your own progress doesn't always have to start with you. One of the most powerful ways to grow in kindness is to celebrate it in the people around you. Did someone extend grace in a hard moment? Did a stranger hold the door a little longer than they had to? Notice it. Name it. Let it inspire you. The more we see kindness, the more we're reminded it's possible. Share it on our Instagram @OutrageousKindess so we can celebrate these acts of kindness with you.

The metrics won't always show up in neat boxes or clean graphs, but you'll feel it. You'll see it in how you respond to challenges. In how you listen. In the moments you pause to count to ten instead of reacting in frustration. In the courage it takes to choose softness when the world expects you to be hard. Kindness compounds, and so does your impact.

WHEN KINDNESS FEELS DIFFICULT

There are days when the world feels sharp and loud, and kindness seems like the last thing you want to offer. Maybe you're tired. Maybe you're overwhelmed or someone has just tested your patience for the tenth time before noon. In those moments, kindness may feel out of reach. How do we stay encouraged when kindness feels hard?

First, we start by knowing ourselves. We all have an "unkind" persona that surfaces under stress as an emotional reflex. Some people get angry or defensive. Others shut down. Some try to solve everything or retreat into silence. Others try to diffuse tension with humor or carry burdens quietly, hoping the moment will pass. None of these responses is wrong per se, but they *are* worth noticing. When we can name our default reactions, we can begin to change them.

Self-awareness is the gateway to kindness. When you understand how you react under pressure, you can build tools to re-center and respond with grace. Sometimes that means pressing pause and taking a breath. Maybe you need to step away from the chaos—not forever, but long enough to come back with a clearer mind and a calmer spirit. Distance can be an act of kindness, too, especially when it prevents us from reacting in ways we'll regret.

Other times, it means acknowledging that you're simply not in the right place—emotionally, mentally, or even physically—to offer kindness right now, and that's OK. Give yourself permission to walk away from situations that repeatedly pull you out of alignment. As a colleague of mine used to say, "It's not my circus, and it's not my monkey." You don't have to stay in environments that bring out the worst in you.

Just don't confuse walking away with failure. Sometimes, choosing peace is the kindest decision you can make for yourself and everyone else. I once walked away from a very high-paying job with lots of perks without really knowing what I would do next. The company culture and core values drained me, I never felt heard, and I couldn't make the changes needed to advance my team. It was not easy to walk away, but I have never regretted it.

Another thing you can do when kindness feels difficult is to reconnect with your *why*. Why did you choose this path in the first place? What impact are you trying to make? What version of yourself are you working toward becoming?

Set small, meaningful goals. Celebrate your progress. Don't grind so hard that you forget to dance a little when things go well. When we lose the joy of the journey, kindness starts to feel like a chore instead of a choice, so mark your milestones, no matter how small. Let them energize you.

Above all else, remember that you're not going to get it right every time. You're going to get tired. You're going to snap. You're going to have car rides like I did recently with my stepdaughter, where road rage bubbles up and you realize you've been stewing in microaggressions for hours. That's not kindness to yourself, and the truth is, it's *you* those little frustrations are eating alive.

Extend the same grace to yourself that you want to extend to others. Be kind to yourself first.

THE PHILANTHROPISTS NEXT DOOR

One thing I've learned after a lifetime of philanthropy is that the size of your bank account says very little about the size of your heart.

We often make assumptions about who gives, how much they give, and what generosity looks like, but some of the most powerful gifts I've ever seen didn't come from boardroom moguls or billionaires with naming rights. They came from humble, everyday people who had built their lives around a different definition of success.

They were, quite simply, the philanthropists next door.

Years ago, I was helping raise $10 million for a campaign to restore a historic church building in Maine. It was an unanticipated follow-up effort. The original campaign had fallen short, mostly because of unexpected renovation costs (anyone who's ever opened a century-old wall knows how quickly budgets can balloon). Some donors were frustrated. Others were skeptical.

And then something unforgettable happened. At a community meeting, a man who ran the local sandwich shop stood up. He was a quiet, working-class guy. He and his two sisters ran a tiny, no-frills place where you could get a turkey sandwich, a slice of bologna, maybe some American cheese, a bag of chips. No lattes, no branding, no Instagrammable aesthetic. Just simple food and friendly service. They lived in the same modest home they grew up in, went to church every Sunday, and worked every day. Theirs was a life of simplicity.

That day, in the middle of all the murmurs and doubt, the man stood up and calmly said, "My family is going to give one million dollars to this campaign."

The room fell silent. A million dollars! From the sandwich shop!

I remember thinking, *You've been selling bologna sandwiches and saving that kind of money?* But of course, that wasn't the full story. They had built their lives around generosity as a core value. They weren't trying to impress anyone. They weren't looking for recognition. They had simply decided that their success would be measured not by what they *kept*, but by what they *gave*.

That gift changed everything. People were inspired. Suddenly, the energy in the room shifted. If the sandwich shop was stepping up, others could too. Their kindness was contagious.

Not long after that, I met another remarkable giver. He was a doctor and a brilliant medical innovator, with multiple patents and a highly successful career. On paper, he seemed like the sort of person you'd expect to see living in luxury, but when I went to visit him and his wife about a charitable project, I found myself in a modest neighborhood, double-checking the address. Their home was simple, even worn. The furniture was decades old. The driveway had an aging car.

What I discovered inside that house was a radical philosophy at work. From the very beginning of their marriage, they had committed to giving away more than they kept. They didn't wait until after they'd "made it," or after the student loans were paid, or the kids were grown. It became their intentional practice from day one. That decision shaped every choice they made, and when it came time to support the cause I was there to discuss, they gave more than a million dollars.

Their story, and the sandwich shop's story, share the same powerful truth: Generosity is not about *abundance* but *mindset*. It's about asking, "What do I have that I can share?" And then answering that question with courage and purpose.

Too often, I hear people say, "I'll give when I make more money," but that moment rarely arrives. The problem is, once you start chasing *enough*, the finish line keeps moving.

Philanthropy, at its best, is about more than writing checks. Ultimately, it's about writing values into the story of your life. It's about living in a way that says, "I may not have everything, but I have more than enough to give."

CREATING YOUR PHILANTHROPY ROAD MAP

Most generous people aren't the ones with the most money, but the ones who've chosen to begin with what they have, from where they are, fueled by what matters to them most. They align their giving with their passions, outrage, and joy, and they start doing it now.

Even Bill Gates admitted this. When he launched the Giving Pledge with Warren Buffett and Melinda French in June 2010, their aim was to encourage the ultrarich to donate the majority of their wealth. At the outset, many billionaires treated major wealth transfers differently from business decisions. Despite being decisive in business, strategic in investments, and data-driven in operations, they often lacked clarity about structuring impactful, thoughtful philanthropy. Most were unclear about how to give.

If giving with intention is hard for billionaires, what hope do the rest of us have?

Plenty, but it starts by getting personal.

1. FIND WHAT MATTERS TO YOU MOST

We each need to build a road map that is *ours* and that begins with paying attention to what moves us. Remember our questions around Impact: What makes you cry? What stirs your anger? What lights you up with joy or inspiration? What do you find yourself returning to, again and again?

Look back on the last month. What headline caught in your throat? What story made you whisper, "This just isn't right?" Was it about injustice, neglect, inequality, or suffering? Was it about hope, healing, nature, or education? These emotional clues aren't random. They're road signs that point you toward what your heart cares most deeply about.

Your giving—whether it's time, money, or attention—should follow that path. If a news story about foster children keeps you up at night, maybe that's where you begin. If hearing about contaminated water sources angers you, explore organizations addressing clean water access. If you laugh out loud in joy watching shelter dogs find new homes, lean into that love of animals. Whether it's arts, education, sustainability, literacy, or veterans' health—there is no wrong answer. Your values are the map.

2. DETERMINE YOUR BANDWIDTH

After you've clarified what moves you, the next question is: What do you have to give? Sometimes it's money. Sometimes it's time. Sometimes it's your platform, your skills, or simply your voice. I've had seasons in my life when I couldn't show up at the gala, couldn't chair the fundraiser, couldn't commit to yet another board. I was caregiving, running a business, trying to keep life afloat, but I could still write a check. I could still use my social media to highlight causes I cared about. I could still *share the good*.

What is realistic for your life *right now*? If you're in the thick of raising a family, managing a business, or juggling multiple obligations, your time may be limited, but that doesn't mean you can't be generous in some way. On the other hand, if you're entering a new chapter—perhaps post-career or newly retired— you have the opportunity to engage in a more significant way. Are you a strategic thinker who loves the big picture? You may thrive on nonprofit boards, where you can offer guidance and vision. Or are you more hands-on, energized by grassroots work and direct service? That clarity can guide not only *where* you give but *how*.

It also helps to consider your personality. Do you love working independently, or do you come alive in community? The book *Seven Faces of Philanthropy* by Russ Alan Prince describes how some people prefer social giving—galas, events, community campaigns—while others are fulfilled by quiet contributions behind the scenes.[24]

There's no one way to be generous. There's only *your* way. The important thing is that you start. Once you've identified what ignites you, take stock of your bandwidth—whether that's an hour a week, a monthly donation, or a single post of advocacy. As your capacity grows, your generosity will grow with it.

At the end of the day, the world doesn't need more wealthy donors. It needs more wholehearted givers.

3. SET YOUR GOALS

Next, consider your desired outcomes. Are you someone who finds meaning in building a specific thing—like a new women's shelter in your town—or do you prefer setting a broader goal, like giving away a certain percentage of your income each year? Some people are content with writing a check and never thinking about it again. Others want impact reports, metrics, and visible change. Neither is better or worse—they're just different styles. The more you know about your expectations, the more aligned your giving will be.

Above all, be patient with yourself. Most people don't know what brings them the deepest joy in giving until they've actually started. Generosity is like any other practice—you learn by doing.

Just remember, there's a lot of pressure on nonprofits to operate with impossibly low overhead. That can make it hard for them to deliver the kind of detailed reporting some donors desire or volunteer experiences that extend beyond stuffing an envelope. Additionally, many of the problems nonprofits are tackling, such as poverty, education gaps, or climate change, don't have quick fixes. You won't solve them with a single donation or in a single year. That doesn't mean your giving doesn't matter. It means you're part of a longer journey toward lasting impact.

If you're especially passionate about a cause but can't find an organization addressing it directly, you may be tempted to start something new. That's a valid path, but it requires careful consideration. Do you truly have the time, energy, and support to build something that extends beyond yourself? Many well-intentioned people launch nonprofits only to realize that it becomes unsustainable when it centers solely on their vision or availability. If you go that route, plan carefully and build for continuity. Make it bigger than you.

4. IDENTIFY KEY RELATIONSHIPS

Another key element of your philanthropic road map is *relationships*. Who do you want to involve in your giving journey? Your spouse or partner? Your kids or grandkids? Your team at work? Sharing your giving decisions, your "why," and your hopes for impact can become a powerful legacy.

Look back. Think about the generosity you witnessed growing up. Did your family model giving? Was it talked about at the dinner table, practiced in quiet ways, or never really discussed at all? Wherever you came from, it's never too late to reflect on what generosity means to *you* and how you want to model it going forward.

Outrageous Kindness is about building a life that reflects your values, passions, and belief that the world gets better when we show up for each other. So take the first step. Name your passion. Check your bandwidth. Set your goals. And decide who's coming with you. That's your road map.

LIVING BELOW YOUR MEANS

One of the most radical, outrageous acts of kindness we can offer, to ourselves and to our communities, is choosing to live below our means. Let's be honest, this idea often meets firm resistance. Many have considered this approach, but the objections usually come quickly: "You don't understand. I have kids to take care of. I've got bills. There's no room left to cut."

The fact is, if you don't start now, you probably never will. There will always be other obligations, always a reason to wait for a better time, but waiting rarely leads to change. Action does.

I know someone who has spent her whole adult life chasing "enough" but never quite catching it. With every raise and every promotion, her lifestyle rises to meet it. Giving, saving, or planning ahead always feels out of reach. She isn't selfish, but she believes that somehow, someday, she will reach a magic place where she has all she needs and then can give generously without other obligations getting in the way.

Financial stress is one of the most common and most corrosive forms of anxiety we carry. The American Psychological Association reports that nearly 72 percent of Americans feel stressed about money at least some of the time.[25] That kind of chronic strain can quietly chip away at your well-being, disrupting sleep, raising blood pressure, and straining relationships. Living below your means won't solve every problem, but it will lower the volume on some of the loudest ones.

This is especially true for parents. The cultural pressure is relentless. Every child must have what every other child has: the newest sneakers, the latest phone, the most expensive birthday party. Sometimes it's easier to resist peer pressure for ourselves than it is for our kids, but that's where a quiet revolution can begin.

When you live below your means and explain why to your children, you give them a value system. You teach them that appearances don't define worth. That self-respect matters more than name brands.

When you consistently spend less than you earn, you build margin, and margin is power. Power to navigate emergencies, to invest in your future, to rest without fear. As Dale Alexander puts it in *The Talk (About Money)*, "Small financial habits, built early and practiced steadily, can lead to massive peace-of-mind dividends."

I learned this firsthand in one of my first jobs out of college, working as a financial adviser. Eager to build confidence, I asked friends of my family to let me practice my sales pitch for annuities and life insurance. One man from our church agreed. He'd worked for the railroad all his life and lived in the modest home his parents had left him. He'd never married or had children. In fact, he seemed like the last person who would need life insurance or have much money to invest. Still, he patiently let me give my presentation, even as I stumbled through it without taking a breath.

Then he surprised me. He started asking tough, technical questions about guaranteed returns, risk profiles, and interest rates. At first, I thought he was just helping me sharpen my skills, but at the end of our meeting, he stunned me again. He told me he wanted to invest a sizable sum in the annuity I had described.

It turned out that years earlier, he'd made a decision to save a fixed percentage of every paycheck, no matter how small. As his income grew, so did the amount he saved, yet he never changed his lifestyle. He lived simply, avoided unnecessary risk, and made consistent, deliberate choices. He became my best client, and to this day, he remains one of my greatest teachers.

His story isn't an outlier. Throughout my career, I've met countless people like him—the "philanthropists next door." They don't look wealthy. Their homes are humble. Their clothes are neat but not flashy. Their children don't have every new gadget. However, behind their simplicity is a profound freedom—a freedom to give and plan for the future instead of fearing it.

So, if you want to adopt this lifestyle, where do you begin?

Start by *noticing*. Track your spending—not to judge yourself, but to understand yourself. Money always tells a story. It reveals what we value, what we fear, what we avoid. Even small insights can spark meaningful change. Today's digital tools make it easier than ever to identify leaks, including those unused subscriptions, impulsive purchases, or habits that no longer serve you.

Then take a *small step*. Maybe it's skipping one coffee shop run per week and setting that money aside. Maybe it's one fewer bottle of wine or one less impulse buy. The goal isn't deprivation but direction. Use what you save to build a buffer. Start a "freedom fund." Create breathing room.

Automate whatever you can. If money moves out of your account before you see it, you won't miss it. That's the genius of workplace retirement plans—money saved before it ever tempts you.

Most importantly, *talk* about money. Make it a values-based conversation with your family. Why are you living this way? What does *enough* mean to you? What matters more than having more? Not every household has these conversations. A friend once described his entire childhood as a series of fights about money. One parent was a spender, the other a saver, and both were locked in perpetual conflict. In the turmoil, even basics like groceries sometimes slipped through the cracks.

We can choose differently. We can create homes where money is discussed with clarity, not fear. Where simplicity is honored. Where generosity flows from intention, not excess. Outrageous Kindness isn't just how we treat others—it's how we manage what we've been given.

Living below your means is not an act of scarcity. It's an act of strength. It's a way to say, "I trust myself. I honor what I have. And I want to live in a way that makes room for others too."

THE KINDNESS OF ONE SIMPLE VIDEO

One of the most radical acts of kindness we can offer is clarity in the face of life's uncertainty. That means making sure the people you love most understand exactly what you want if you become too sick to care for yourself or if you pass away. Making your healthcare, end-of-life, and after-death wishes unmistakably clear is not about preparing for death; it's about protecting life, especially the lives of those who will carry on after you.

Dr. Frank Harrington, longtime pastor of Peachtree Presbyterian Church in Atlanta, spent decades walking beside families in their most vulnerable hours, in grief-stricken hospital rooms, at tearful funerals, and in uncertain waiting rooms. Over the years, he noticed that the deepest stress and conflict often came not from the loss itself but from the lack of clarity. Families who had once been close suddenly found themselves divided and confused, struggling to agree on what their loved one would have wanted.

From that insight, Dr. Harrington began sharing a simple but powerful practice. He recommended recording a video of just a few minutes in which you speak directly to your loved ones. Do it while you're healthy. Tell them what you want and share what matters to you. Let them hear your voice, your calmness, your love, and tell them you trust them. It might seem small, but the impact can be profound.

When Dr. Harrington first told me about this idea, he had just finished recording his own video. He didn't know it then, but he would pass away not long after. When I got the news, I remember thinking, *He left a video. He left peace and clarity.* That's Outrageous Kindness—thinking ahead and taking five minutes to ease the burden on others.

When someone you love is dying or in crisis, you're caught in a whirlwind of fear, heartache, and confusion. The last thing anyone should have to do at that moment is *guess,* or worse, *argue.* Should you be kept on life support? Who should speak for you if you can't speak for yourself? Do you want a memorial? What kind? These are not easy questions, but when they're answered in advance, what could have been chaos becomes peace.

I know this from experience. When my father was first diagnosed with Alzheimer's, my brother and oldest sister stepped in to help our mother navigate what came next. They met with an attorney and updated all the essential documents: wills, healthcare proxies, and advance directives. I still laugh at how, after that meeting, my mother calmly told each of us kids what we'd be receiving, and then turned to me and said, with a smile, "You'll be the one to pull the plug."

It was funny at the time, but it was also real. Years later, that role became more than theoretical. My father entered hospice care, with my mother faithfully by his side. Then, in a cruel twist, just about a year later, she suffered a sudden heart attack. The doctors weren't sure if she would recover. At first, she was alert enough to speak, and I called everyone. My brother drove over twelve hours, and some friends traveled hundreds of miles. In those last forty-eight hours, my mother had sacred, final conversations with each of us. Then, she declined quickly.

Even though we had everything documented, even though we *knew* her wishes, there was still that ache to hold on. My siblings and I clung to hope, looking for reasons to delay the inevitable. And then, when I tried to help her take her medication, she gently grabbed my hand and whispered just one word: "Don't."

She reminded me of the promise, and because of her clarity, I had the courage to honor it. We were able to love her not just with our words, but with our choices.

I would face it again, just two years later. When my husband—my business partner, best friend, and the father of our son—was diagnosed with Lewy body dementia, it felt like a death sentence with no mercy. Fortunately, we had already done the hard work of planning when I was the one facing a breast cancer diagnosis. We'd had the conversations, and now, as his illness progressed, I was grateful we had.

He told me clearly: no machines, no feeding tubes. He wanted to stay home as long as possible. He wanted dignity. Keeping him at home was not easy. There were days of confusion, hallucinations, and utter exhaustion. With our son still in middle school, the weight of caregiving grew too heavy. Eventually, we made the painful decision to move him into a care home. His decline was rapid. Soon, he could no longer eat or swallow, and I remembered again what he had said: *no tubes*. It broke my heart, but honoring his wishes was how I showed my love and valued his love for his family.

Hospice helped. Close friends carried us. While nothing about it was easy, it would have been unbearable without the clarity we had. These moments have shaped how I view kindness. Sometimes, it isn't soft. Sometimes, it shows up in legal documents and hard conversations. Sometimes, kindness is making a promise and keeping it when it's hardest.

I'm not the only one who believes this. The National Institute on Aging confirms that advance directives reduce family conflict and increase peace of mind (NIA, 2022). Studies published in *JAMA* and *BMJ Supportive & Palliative Care* show that clear directives dramatically reduce emotional trauma for surviving family members.

Kindness doesn't always look like charity or service. Sometimes it looks like preparation. Sometimes it sounds like a quiet, steady voice on a video saying, "I love you. I trust you. Here's what I hope for."

WHAT YOU CAN DO RIGHT NOW

It's one thing to understand the importance of making your wishes known. It's another thing entirely to take action. Thankfully, you don't have to have everything figured out to begin. You just need to take one small, courageous step.

Start by putting a few essential documents in place. These are acts of kindness, clarity, and care for the people you love most.

- **Will**—This outlines how your assets should be distributed and can also include your preferences for a funeral or memorial service.
- **Durable Power of Attorney for Healthcare**—Sometimes called a healthcare proxy, this names someone you trust to make medical decisions for you if you can't make them yourself.
- **Living Will or Advance Directive**—This expresses your wishes for medical interventions like CPR, ventilators, or feeding tubes, so your loved ones aren't left guessing.
- **Durable Power of Attorney for Finances**—This appoints someone to handle your financial matters if you're unable to do so yourself.

These documents are not set in stone. Life evolves, so do relationships, priorities, and possibilities. Review these plans once a year—on your birthday, at the start of a new year, or any date you'll remember. Update them as needed. Most importantly, make sure your loved ones know what's been updated and where to find the documents when it matters most.

If you want to go one step further, as mentioned earlier, record a short video. Speak directly to the people you love. Tell them your wishes. Tell them what matters to you. Tell them you trust them. It doesn't need to be polished or formal.

In moments of stress or uncertainty, hearing your steady, loving voice can be a powerful anchor. It's not just a legal tool. It's an emotional compass.

After all, sometimes, Outrageous Kindness is making the hardest conversations easier for the people you love, even when you're gone.

Tools for Practicing Outrageous Kindness

Practice Daily Kindness Habits:
- Ask for help, input, or connection every day.
- Thank someone meaningfully each day.
- Highlight and amplify the good in others.

Build Community Through Invitation:
- Invite people into shared experiences and moments of togetherness.

Use Your Voice and Platform for Good:
- Share stories of kindness, repost uplifting content, and promote causes you care about.

Create and Follow your Personal Kindness Road Map:
- Identify what moves you emotionally and aligns with your values.
- Determine your bandwidth (time, money, voice) and give accordingly.

- Set specific, meaningful generosity goals and revisit them regularly.

Live Below Your Means to Create Margin for Generosity:

- Track spending, reduce unnecessary expenses, and automate saving and giving.
- Have honest, values-based conversations about money with your family.

Leave a Legacy of Clarity and Care:

- Complete essential legal documents (will, health-care proxy, living will, power of attorney).
- Record a short video to communicate your wishes directly to loved ones.
- Review and update plans annually, and ensure others know where to find them.

Outrageous Kindness Is a Piece of Cake

KINDNESS SOUNDS BEAUTIFUL in theory. In reality, it's often messy, complicated, and uncomfortable. It asks more of us than we think we have to give, especially when life itself has already stretched us thin.

April 18, 2020, was one of those days for me. I woke up determined to have a "normal" day, as normal as anything could be during the early weeks of a global pandemic and the fresh, raw grief of losing my husband. The morning was productive enough. I answered emails, handled a few personal tasks, and even squeezed in a little exercise. It gave me a brief, fragile sense of control.

And then *she* showed up at my door. The young woman had been to my house many times before because she was part of the team that helped clean our home, but I hadn't seen her in almost two months. Since the pandemic had begun, we hadn't discussed her returning, and certainly not on this particular day.

At first, I was just surprised. But then I noticed the differences. She was alone. Her car wasn't in the driveway. She wore a hospital bracelet and a pandemic mask. And there, around her neck, were chain-like bruise marks, dark and raw.

Scared of COVID, unsure of the risks, I hesitated. I opened the door just a crack, apologized that I couldn't invite her in, and listened. Through frantic tears, she pieced together her story:

She had walked two miles from the hospital to my home because she didn't know where else to go. Her boyfriend had choked her with a chain and beaten her. Neighbors had gotten her to the hospital, but she was terrified that if she stayed there, she would either be sent away or somehow returned to the man who hurt her. Her boss was the mother of her abuser. She had no safe haven, no trusted person to call, and no clear way forward.

Even on my best day, I'm not sure I would have known exactly what to do, but that day, as I was grieving and tired in the middle of a pandemic, I felt completely overwhelmed. My first instinct was to simply make her feel safe. I offered her a chair on the front porch and brought her a glass of water and the only comfort I could quickly find: a piece of cake.

It sounds small, almost laughably small compared to the gravity of what she had endured, but the cake was all I had to give at that moment. After a series of Easter storms and power outages, combined with my deep reluctance to face grocery stores during COVID and the lingering paralysis of grief, my supplies were dwindling. That piece of cake was the last remnant of a meal I had shared with loved ones after my husband's memorial service.

There's something almost poetic about it. Twice before in my life, cake had been the last thing left in the refrigerator during major life upheavals. After Hurricane Hugo ripped through Charlotte, North Carolina, when I was temporarily living there,

OUTRAGEOUS KINDNESS IS A PIECE OF CAKE

all that remained was a piece of frozen cake and a can of Sprite. Years later, as I packed up my house following a divorce, I found once again a lone piece of frozen cake.

Ironically, I don't even like cake that much. I prefer the frosting, but somehow, in life's most broken, empty moments, cake seems to be what remains.

That morning, while this woman picked at the cake, I went inside and called a friend who also knew the cleaning crew. Through tears, we caught up briefly on my husband's passing. Then she confirmed what I already suspected: This wasn't the first time the young woman's boyfriend had been violent, and she had no supportive family member to call.

Together, we brainstormed services that might help her, but the list was heartbreakingly short. Over and over again in the coming hours, I would hear the same devastating sentence: "We don't have a shelter here."

I knew I didn't have the emotional strength alone to figure out the next steps, but I also knew she couldn't go back to the life she had fled. That night, she slept in our guest house. Later, my stepdaughter came to help, bringing calm and presence when mine was running thin. Together, we gently encouraged her to talk to a sheriff's deputy who could connect her with the support services she needed. Eventually, she agreed to press charges. The deputy patiently listened and stayed until she felt safe enough to take that brave step.

It was not neat or easy. It wasn't a storybook rescue. It was messy and hard and full of fear and uncertainty, but it was kindness. And it started with knowing more—taking the time to listen, to set aside my fear, and to see her not through assumptions or quick judgments, but through compassion.

Outrageous Kindness isn't about having perfect answers. It's about showing up, knowing enough to care, and caring enough to act, even if, sometimes, all you have to offer is a piece of cake and an open door.

Ultimately, the KIND Method is more than a set of principles—it's a way of living and leading with intention. *Know more* invites us to stay curious and humble, expanding our awareness through listening and reflection. *Impact* anchors our purpose in measurable change, turning ideals into tangible outcomes. *Navigate* gives us the resilience to stay aligned through uncertainty, while *Deliver* reminds us that follow-through is where transformation truly happens. Finally, *Dance* gives us the freedom to express joy through it all.

And in a world that often feels divided and distracted, choosing to lead with kindness through small, consistent acts has the power to quietly, steadily, and profoundly change the world.

So, let's get started.

Become Part of the Movement

We're building a global movement of people who believe kindness can be a force for change. Changing one million lives with one outrageously kind mission. Join us on the journey at OutrageousKindness.com.

ACKNOWLEDGMENTS

FIRST AND FOREMOST, my deepest thanks to Susan Boyette—a fellow godass (goddess + badass = godass), a friend of more than twenty-five years, my business partner, and a true creative thought partner in bringing this book to life. Her remarkable memory for stories I'd long forgotten, her unwavering support, and her presence through every season of my life have been invaluable. She's been a surrogate aunt to my son, a steady anchor through life's ups and downs, and, in the most heartfelt and humorous way, my late husband's "other wife"—a title she earned through decades of deep friendship, fierce loyalty, and unconditional love. Susan has been part of our family in every way that counts—and then some.

A heartfelt thank you to the incredible team at Streamline, especially Jeff Miller, who somehow took my scattered stories and helped shape them into something that actually made sense, without ever dimming the creative spark.

To Whitney McDuff and Erin Thomas at the Whitter Group— thank you for sitting with me for hours, asking the right questions, and helping draw the vision of Outrageous Kindness and the KIND Method out of me. Your clarity, care, and commitment brought it fully to life.

To our official chief ambassador of Outrageous Kindness, Cynthia Bolden—thank you for your boundless energy, visionary spirit, and ability to dream even bigger dreams for this movement than I sometimes can. And to our very first Outrageous Kindness Pledge-taker, friend, and connector extraordinaire, Brooke Krizbal—thank you for your boldness and belief.

Rachel Parks, Caki Field, and Tanner McCraney—thank you for your insight, expertise, and willingness to teach an old dog new tricks.

To Bob Carter, Neal White, Angela Atkins, John T. Edge, and the ever-amazing Beth Ann Fennelly—thank you for your creativity that inspires me (and the world), and for your generous time and guidance as we shaped how to share this message with new audiences.

To the friends who always say yes—whether it's time for an adventure or to blow off steam with a yellow ball—thank you for keeping me grounded and laughing.

And to the Outrageous Kindness community—you are the lifeblood of this book. The world needs you now more than ever. You are already making change, and there's so much more to come.

ABOUT THE AUTHOR

KRISTINA JOY CARLSON is a globally recognized philanthropy expert, entrepreneur, and purpose-driven leader with more than thirty years of experience in fundraising, leadership, and impact strategy. She has helped guide transformational campaigns, secure eight-figure philanthropic gifts, raise billions of dollars, and craft innovative approaches for some of the world's most influential organizations, including Habitat for Humanity International, Special Olympics, Susan G. Komen, and Boys & Girls Clubs of America.

As the Founder and CEO of Outrageous Kindness and creator of the KIND Method, Kristina empowers individuals, organizations, and communities to lead with intention, generosity, and bold action. Her work has supported the philanthropic visions of former US presidents, Fortune 500 CEOs, faith leaders, celebrities, and everyday changemakers.

Kristina's passion for impact is deeply personal. While navigating executive leadership, she also walked through nearly a decade of caregiving, profound grief, and her own battle with cancer. These experiences shaped her core belief: that no matter the adversity we face, we each have the power to lead with purpose and spark meaningful change.

A best-selling author and sought-after speaker, Kristina invites readers to reimagine kindness not as a soft sentiment but as a strategic force for good. Through compelling storytelling and hard-won wisdom, she inspires us all to build lives rooted in purpose—and to change the world one small, intentional act at a time.

Endnotes

1   Mike Shedlock, "Gen Z, the Most Pessimistic Generation in History, May Decide the Election," MishTalk, March 15, 2024, https://mishtalk.com/economics/gen-z-the-most-pessimistic-generation-in-history-may-decide-the-election/.

2   Raj Chetty, Will Dobbie, Benjamin Goldman, Sonya R. Porter, and Crystal S. Yang, "Changing Opportunity: Sociological Mechanisms Underlying Growing Class Gaps and Shrinking Race Gaps in Economic Mobility," NBER Working Paper No. 32697 (National Bureau of Economic Research, July 2024).

3   Richard Kestenbaum, "The Beauty Business Keeps Growing But It's Missing a Huge Opportunity," Forbes, June 27, 2024, citing Euromonitor International data that show global beauty-industry revenue reached $570 billion in 2023.

4 Erica Chenoweth and Maria J. Stephan, Why Civil Resistance Works: The Strategic Logic of Nonviolent Conflict (Columbia University Press, 2011).

5 Archy O. de Berker et al., "Computations of Uncertainty Mediate Acute Stress Responses in Humans," Nature Communications 7 (2016): Article 10996, https://doi.org/10.1038/ncomms10996.

6 Marlynn Wei, "How High Performers Overcome Decision Fatigue," Psychology Today, April 8, 2025, https://www.psychologytoday.com/us/blog/urban-survival/202503/maximizing-decisions-how-high-performers-overcome-decision-fatigue.

7 C. Antón, "The Impact of Role Stress on Workers' Behaviour Through Job Satisfaction and Organizational Commitment," International Journal of Psychology 44, no. 3 (2009): 187–194.

8 "Elevating Achievement," Georgia State University News, accessed June 12, 2025, https://news.gsu.edu/magazine/elevating-achievement.

9 Edward N. Lorenz, "Predictability: Does the Flap of a Butterfly's Wings in Brazil Set Off a Tornado in Texas?" 1972 conference of the American Association for the Advancement of Science, Washington, DC.

10 www.dci.org.

11 Douglas M. Lawson, Give to Live: How Giving Can Change Your Life (Alti Publishing, 1998).

12 Rush University Medical Center, "The Health Benefits of Giving," accessed June 7, 2025, https://www.rush.edu/news/health-benefits-giving.

13 Dale Alexander, "The Talk" (About Money): A Young Adult's Guide to the One Decision That Changes Everything (pub. by author, 2022).

14 ABC7 News, "FedEx Founder Fred Smith, Marine Corps Veteran, Revolutionized Package Delivery, Dies at 80," ABC7, June 21, 2025, https://abc7.com/post/fedex-founder-fred-smith-marine-corps-veteran-revolutionized-package-delivery-dies-80/16830938/.

15 Moneycontrol. "Gen Z Prioritizes Job Satisfaction over Salary: Survey," April 30, 2024, https://www.moneycontrol.com/news/business/gen-z-prioritises-job-satisfaction-over-salary-survey-12532471.html; Edelman. 2018 Edelman Earned Brand Report: Brands Take a Stand. October 2018, https://www.edelman.com/research/earned-brand-2018.

16 Marcus Buckingham, Go Put Your Strengths to Work: 6 Powerful Steps to Achieve Outstanding Performance (Free Press, 2007).

17 Luke 5:17–26.

18 Robert Waldinger and Marc Schulz, "What the Longest Study on Human Happiness Found Is the Key to a Good Life," The Atlantic, January 19, 2023.

19 Mark Twain, Autobiography of Mark Twain, ed. Harriet Elinor Smith and the Editors of the Mark Twain Project (University of California Press, 2010), 276.

20 Panteleimon-Dimitriou "Pan" Punnet, "Lack of Enjoyment Reduces the Motivation to Succeed in Sport," Journal of Sports Sciences 34, no. 1 (2016): 45–53.

21 A. T. Kearney, Joy at Work: Exploring the "Joy Gap" in Global Organizations (A. T. Kearney, 2018), 1–2.

22 "Finding Joy in Black Philanthropy," AFPGlobal.org

23 Ting Ting Tan et al., "Mindful Gratitude Journaling: Psychological Distress, Quality of Life and Suffering in Advanced Cancer: A Randomised Controlled Trial," BMJ Supportive & Palliative Care 13, no. e2 (2023): e389; Robert A. Emmons and Michael E. McCullough, "Counting Blessings versus Burdens: An Experimental Investigation of Gratitude and Subjective Well-Being in Daily Life," Journal of Personality and Social Psychology 88, no. 2 (2005): 377–89; Irene A. Althaus et al., "Gratitude among Advanced Cancer Patients and Their Caregivers: Associations with Quality of Life and Psychological Distress," Frontiers in Oncology 12 (2022): 991250.

24 Russ Alan Prince and Karen Maru File, Seven Faces of Philanthropy: A New Approach to Cultivating Major Donors (Jossey-Bass, 1994).

25 American Psychological Association, "APA's 2015 Stress in America Survey Found That 72 Percent of Americans Reported Feeling Stressed about Money at Least Some of the Time in the Prior Month," in Speaking of Psychology podcast, February 4, 2015.

www.ingramcontent.com/pod-product-compliance
Lightning Source LLC
Chambersburg PA
CBHW071644210326
41597CB00017B/2115